WE
BLEW
IT

HOW AMERICA HAD FUN
LOSING EVERYTHING

BARRY R. NORMAN

WE BLEW IT

FOREWORD by Rick Schmidt

As I read Barry Norman's new book, *We Blew It*, beginning with actor/director Dennis Hopper and how his Easy Rider movie impacted my generation's counter-culture, it suddenly occurred to me that since I had actually met the man, a rebel icon of my generation, I might have some first-hand "blowing it" material to contribute (more about this later). With that thought, my mind returned to the 1960s and certain historical events in Berkeley, CA that I'd experienced first-hand. Maybe this could be a good place to start.

BLOWING IT #1

Two years before the debacle of Kent State and a year before the well-known People's Park riots, Spring, 1969, there was a lesser-known "disturbance," June 30, 1968, on Telegraph Avenue. Wikipedia says it was for TWLF (Third World Liberation Front), demanding an end to colonialization by the US and in support of oppressed people everywhere. I got wind of something going on between cops and U.C. students and that it was taking place during a city-wide curfew. It was happening about a mile from my apartment on Russell Street, and I Ifelt I had to check it out. It was already dark when I spotted an armed National Guard soldier on the corner a block ahead. I returned home, added a black T-shirt to my black jeans (thinking ninja?), and traveled through the centers of the blocks to get there.

Emerging at Telegraph and Dwight Way, I found myself part of a group of maybe 100 equally young people (I was 25), the street ahead cordoned off with at least 50 National Guard troops and Berkeley cops lined up in riot gear. I was relieved to be at the back of my crowd, feeling protected by all the bodies between me and soldiers. But suddenly I heard a noise from behind. Spinning around I was shocked to see another whole bunch of uniforms—I was now in the front row! Before I could think holy shit a teargas canister hit about halfway between us, fumes spraying toward my eyes. The very next second a young guy near me shouted, "Follow me to the roof! We'll be safe there!" Half-blinded, I trailed him and others up a smokey staircase. On top we could see the mostly empty Ave., heading back toward my Russell Street, Ashby Avenue farther down. And we watched.

In the chaos I saw a young couple approach a cop, just past where the original Krishna Copy store was located. By their body language it seemed that they were innocents—collegiate clothes, straight short hair on the man, people just caught in the mess. The woman unclenched her hand from her partner and walked over to where the officer was standing, while her friend stayed back. In any case, her body language broadcast, "Hello officer. Please tell us the best way to exit (like my *Dick and Jane* book advertised in the 1950s—Let the friendly policeman help you cross the street). Wrong. The cop immediately struck the woman on the head with his wooden club. She went down hard. Instinctively, her boyfriend ran in to defend her, and three additional cops jumped him, clubbing him to the ground. I can't tell you how my other fellow "rioters" felt watching this, but I was sickened and shocked. Seeing such unwarranted brutality was some kind of defining moment about the dangers of a police state.

BLOWING IT #2 (from my front-row seat).

In '69 my first wife, unbeknownst to me, had signed us up to be part of something in Berkeley called "The Free Church." What that meant was, each night a couple of strangers—usually hippie-looking men, sometimes women—would crash in our small apartment which we shared with two daughters from her first marriage and our two-year-old. One morning I walked out of the bedroom to find two straight-looking men in the front living room, coats on, one of them standing before an open drawer that was part of a built-in cabinet. Half-awake, I didn't think to ask, "What are you looking for," before he said, "Just looking for some other records." OK, I thought. Who cares. I didn't think anything of it. They left and I headed out to buy some milk. Outside the market, in the newspaper stand that held the Berkeley Barb newpapers, I was shocked to see the faces of those two men staring out from the front page. The bold headline read: "Wanted, Dead or Alive: Beware/FBI Agents." Question: Why were young guys, basically my age, snooping around, trying to investigate or bust their fellow citizens?

BLOWING IT #3

When my first marriage fell apart, I found an cheap room to rent in a brown-shingle house (bathroom down the hall), a couple blocks from my Oakland art college. Rent: $20/month. Now, with inflation from 1969, that amount in 2022 dollars would equal $151.94 (so says Google). Try to find a room in the Bay Area (anywhere!) for that little today. Look on Craig's List. The best deal you'd find is probably around $500.

And the landlord let me lower my rent by $2 for each hour I worked in his upholstery shop, (that equates to $15.19/hr. in 2022 dollars). So I could lower my rent 10% by working ONE hour. Nowadays, if rent was $1000, that would mean you'd be getting $100/hr. working off a tenth of the rent. Not bad pay!

Back in '69 a person could live & attend college, even eat(!) on much less. Where did all the livability go? Well, maybe check the cost of our US Military Budget, extracted from yearly Tax Revenue (3.71 trillion in 2020). Approximately 725 billion currently goes to the military (hidden costs may jam this cost much hiigher than reported). Russia spends 61 billion/yr. Google Q&A states: "Reports from the Inspector Generals' offices of Iraq and Afghanistan estimate that the

U.S. military has lost $60 billion to waste and fraud in Iraq, $100 billion to Afghan reconstruction efforts, and billions more in wasted equipment either burned or left behind after the withdrawal of forces." Does this qualify as "blowing it?" I think so. Our quality of life has been shit-canned with such blunders and military waste.

BLOWING IT #4

Back to Dennis Hopper and meeting him. I'd been flown in to The Netherlands, at the Rotterdam film festival, 1977, to premiere my second feature film, *Showboat 1988—The Remake*. It was in middle of the night, in a deserted hallway, 9-hours ahead for me traveling from the California Coast. I had just premiered my early-but-not-final-cut and was walking it off. When we met he was dressed like a cowboy—maybe still living in Taos, New Mexico—broad-brimmed hat, vest, boots. And excuse me for this plug for the film, but the first words out of his mouth were, "Showboat's a great film." Caught in a half-witted, jet-lagged zone, I replied, "You mean the original?" His answer, "No, yours."

After that, he began to (what-I-can-only-call-it) whine, about having to go upstairs to support an Ethiopian director's feature film. OK, I thought, good luck. But the way he spoke—so weak and unsure—triggered my indie-filmmaker angst. Without any restraint I suddenly blurted out the following.

"Wait a minute! You're Dennis Hopper. You've made the most successful independent movie of all time, Easy Rider! Just go up and tell those people you're going to start your own festival. And you'll pick whoever *you want*...Because you're DENNIS HOPPER!"

I guess I felt like if Dennis was this ineffectual, as a winner (a HUGE winner), then what hope was there for any of the rest of us, we filmmaker-unknowns?

Yes, this last example of blowing it may be a bit too abstract for some to understand (a temporarily weak filmmaker...who cares?). It does make me wonder, though, how a (pardon-the-expression) lowly German pencil-maker in Michael Moore's movie, Where To Invade

Next, has a bigger, more secure ego than a miracle-working, famous actor/filmmaker like Dennis Hopper. What is wrong here in the USA? Does this incident I experienced represent something about the low-level of appreciation this country has for The Artist? You bet.

My last one, BLOWING IT #5, is fairly short and sweet.

In May, 1968, I took off on a hitchhike trip to the East Coast from Berkeley. My sign, "EAST COAST OR BUST," finally got me a ride from the on-ramp of Highway 80 at Ashby Ave. The driver, a sales-man-looking guy maybe in his mid-thirties, was silent for the first ten miles or so before he spoke up.

"Why are all of you doing this?" he asked, out of the blue. I tried to digest the question. He seemed to be requiring that I explain *my entire hippie generation*. Actually, I wasn't that hippied-out myself: mustache (not-long hair), P-coat, suitcase and backpack.

My next thought was, This guy is "Mr. Jones!" Like in the Dylan song, *Ballad of a Thin Man*, the lyrics had come alive: "Because something is happening here, but you don't know what it is... Do you, Mr. Jones?"

Anyway, I don't remember answering him. Maybe I just said, Don't know, to get him off my back. No more conversation was to be had. This first hitchhike, one of many to follow, ended with my drop-off near the Lawrence Livermore National Laboratory, home of still-going secret military weapons development.

All in all, Barry Norman's book is certainly way overdue. He covers the spectrum of past, present, and future BLOWING IT, hoping to contribute to a turn of the tide. Someone has to try! Of course none of us may be either intelligent enough or effective enough to turn any of these police-state, unaffordable-living, run-away military industrial complex spending, unappreciated artists things around. But, at least we can keep our eyes open to the world we currently inhabit. And hopefully we can stop blowing it, at least with regard to our own little lives. Thanks Barry!

EASY RIDER

Easy Rider was released on July 14, 1969. As the 60s decade was in its closing months, an independent, road drama in which the keys to the film were given to lunatics Peter Fonda and Dennis Hooper made total sense, although to whom remains a mystery. The defining counterculture film of the 60s, considered to be the first blockbuster of the emerging genre, led to a plethora of rebellious youth films, destroying the idea of who should actually make films and blowing up any ideas of what films outside the studio system could be. The use of edgy rock and roll in the soundtrack and actors who were actually consuming the drugs depicted was an eviscerating *"fuck you"* to the gaggle of beach movies starring Annette Funicello, Frankie Avalon, and Harvey Lembeck's Marlon Brando wannabe. James Dean might have been the cinematic birth of cool, but he lived at home in *Rebel Without a Cause* and Daddy was better known as Mr. Magoo and Thurston Howell III— and his mom played the aforementioned rebel Eddie Haskell's mother in the gritty, 60s TV staple, *Leave it to Beaver*. Fuck you, indeed.

Easy Rider also brought the now legendary Jack Nicholson to the forefront. He would star in *The Last Detail* and *Chinatown* soon after. But it is Peter Fonda's Wyatt/Captain America morosely saying to Dennis Hopper's Billy, "We blew it," that marks the place from which we mine the past, present, and future. Much had been written and said about what we may have blown, other than the obvious. For two characters whose appearance and attitude represented a veritable laundry list of Groucho Marxism, "Whatever It Is, I'm Against It," anti-establishmentisms, getting your brains redistributed all over the highway by two guys who wouldn't be out of place in the hills of *Deliverance* or a Trump rally doesn't seem to be too far-fetched. After all, how much more "establishment" can you get than having your biggest accomplishment be to score a motorcycle cylinder full of cocaine, giving two more apropos uses for the term *blow*? Nothing says "fed up with the system" better than a drug deal gone bad. Unless it's a drug deal gone good, with the protagonist being a high school teacher/cancer patient for whom we'll actually root when he shoots the shit out of a house full of Nazi white supremacists (and the drug is cocaine's child-molesting uncle).

I would say I've digressed, but one would actually have to have a point in order to digress from it. I'm not sure if this is going to be a screed or a manifesto—both literary devices used to describe an adult tantrum. The point is that everything has been devolving into a Devo Boogie Boy's nightmare landscape. George Miller's original remake of *Mad Max* had a more optimistic outlook than I do. But talk to any disaffected alta cocker from any generation and they'll say the same thing about the present: today sucks, yesterday was way better, tomorrow's not even guaranteed, and Goddammit, someone's to blame—and we better find out who, so we can at least short-sheet his bed, or force her to watch a marathon of *The Lawrence Welk Show* with her eyes pried open like Alexander DeLarge in *A Clockwork Orange*. You see, when things suck so bad, you can actually contradict yourself in the same sentence—such as saying how great things were while then naming a hit TV show from that period as a form of torture. Shit gets complicated.

Maybe this is a promulgation. That sounds unnecessarily obtuse, which makes it perfect for these purposes. I can post that on social media and get a shit-ton of likes and shares and possibly land someone in Facebook jail for a *Community Standard* violation. Maybe this is a communiqué. That sounds properly foreign, which will gain a lot of attention amongst both friends and enemies—and YouTubers.

I actually lack the academic background to write any of those things. I'm not a famous *Monty Python* historian, and my opinions aren't being sought by media trolls looking for a pithy quote to validate their nonsense. I have worked in the music, television, and film industries, but that's only helpful for all the pop culture references I'll be making throughout as a substitute for actual knowledge. Truth be known, I'm just a guy with time on his hands—but you don't read Hemingway or Kerouac because you believe them to be boring and you're just looking for some way to pass the time and make a buck.

Screw that. It's time we named names and kicked ass. *Easy Rider* came out in the middle of 1969, so we'll make sure that the line in the sand and everything that happened before didn't count. So right there, we're eliminating both World Wars, The Depression, the triumvirate of political assassinations (but not the rock star trifecta), most of the Civil Rights, Anti-War, and Women's Rights Movements, but we're leaving in disco, so it all evens out. And we won't mention Woodstock. I wasn't there, but I could claim to have been, as about half a million other posers do. It didn't happen, and if it did, no one was watching, and the movie was edited by Scorsese, so the whole thing was an unreliable narration. Besides, Dennis Hopper introduced flash-forward editing, and that's exactly what is happening here—*Easy Rider* flashed forward to the concept of understanding about the collective "*we blew it*," as Peter Fonda foreshadowed.

So I'm going to pop a bunch of Aracept and wash it down with Red Bull to jog my memory and come up with all the tribulations that were behind the current shit-storm. And by the end, we'll all know who or what blew it for all of us, so break out your torches and pitchforks.

THE MOON LANDING CONSPIRACY

NASA landed a man on the moon on July 20, 1969, which means we are skipping over much of the year and claiming that nothing of historic note happened in the six months prior that caused us to "blow it." I might get back to some events such as Stonewall, the erection of the Twin Towers, Woodstock, and Charles Manson, but the moon landing should be placed on the "wow" spectrum (for now), so it's a good place to start. With only six days separating the release of *Easy Rider* and the moon landing, shit was getting real

Neil Armstrong's words, "That's one small step for man...one giant leap for mankind," should have been the high-water mark for American Exceptionalism. We beat Boris and Natasha there, and if ever there was a moment where natural-born enemies hugged each other more than in the ending of *Major League,* that was it.

But noooooooooooooo!!

Instead, we got a boatload of conspiracy theories. Over 400,000 men and women worked for NASA and their various contractors, and they all helped make Mercury and Apollo missions go, but due to their government affiliations, you can't trust them, so it all must have been fake.

That American flag was waving when there was no wind on the moon? FAKE!

Couldn't see any stars in the lunar sky? FAKE!

Those shadows didn't look right to me. FAKE!

Hey! I couldn't see Neil Armstrong's face in the picture he took of Buzz Aldrin. FAKE!

Stanley Kubrick shot the whole thing on a soundstage! Hmmm. This is already the second time Kubrick's name has come up, so it has to be FAKE! Really fake.

So what could have been a bigger cause for the blewdom than having one of the grandest achievements in American and human history been nothing but a con? It was just a conspiracy to make us feel good about ourselves and distract us from Vietnam, Civil Rights, and all of the other major battles raging through the country at that time. Feeling good about ourselves in America was much better when it came through illegal drugs and legal alcohol, nicotine, and divorce, not because of some lame parlor trick. We were so pissed off at life, we couldn't get it up anymore, except for a phony rocket ship that supposedly landed on a Dean Martin pizza pie metaphor. That wasn't *amore*—that was bullshit! Not all cons were considered equal. Tricky Dick hadn't perpetrated his biggest scam yet, although having interfered in the 1968 Peace Talks and not getting called out for it was a good one.

The lies of Vietnam came more and more to the fore in the 70s and had a lot to do with the mistrust or dislike of the government for what they were telling us, often contradicted by journalists reporting from the jungle. Those who kept screaming that the landing was FAKE generally knew that it wasn't, but wanted to give the middle finger to the world at large and anyone who went along with the status quo. They needed to let everyone know just how fucking hurt they were. Some of them were innocents, while others were rubes and people with little sophistication, but all felt left out and had a need to *do something*. Trumpism was the mental and morale condition grandfathered in from their hurt.

But with any conspiracy theory, enough people bought into the idea that the moon landing was hokum to piss in our Cheerios. The thirty-billion-dollar hoodwinkery was concocted just to keep the dollars rolling into NASA, they believed, while enabling our collective souls to save face regarding those nasty Russkies After all, Sputnik was the first ass-whooping we took in the Space Race, and then our German scientists couldn't get a rocket up any better than bad porn worked on the perpetually impotent. When the conspiracy beats the legend, believe the conspiracy.

But what if the conspiracy *WAS* the conspiracy?

What if there has always existed an underground group of conspiracy theorists, like the Masons or the Illuminati or NY Jets fans? They have their secret handshakes and meetings, cooking up the most preposterous ideas about how or why something couldn't be true just to gaslight actual sane people? They probably came up with the word gaslight just to make it a self-fulfilling prophecy. Who else would have made the 1944 movie, *Gaslight,* just so they could make it a regular ritual from then on?

If you constantly poke holes into everything, the rest of us don't have enough fingers to plug up the dyke. What we need is a group of anti-conspiracy theorists to invent even more convoluted reasons why the CTs should be debunked. You could even combine a couple, just to screw with their heads.

The Earth is flat *and* the moon landings never happened? Fine. Then we were actually able to use the Flat Earth as a giant springboard to launch astronauts to the moon like Rodney Dangerfield performing the death-defying Triple Lindy. And dammit if they didn't stick the landing. Turns out that the Earth is actually made of *Flubber*, so pick your poison of which silliness to debunk first. Come up with a better Rube Goldberg contraption that could explain it and we might just believe you. But probably not. You can't even produce any Bigfoot fossils or scat, and you believe they currently walk the Earth.

Earth-jumping has actually been a proposed Olympic event for decades, just barely missing out from being added to the 1976, Montreal Games, 1988 Calgary Games, and the 2010 Games in Vancouver. But Aarschot, Belgium has been readying a proposal and, if awarded the Games, they have promised to make Earth-jumping an official event, along with beer pong, tetherball, and the combo of curling/bowling where the athlete never lets go of the rock as it goes hurtling down the alley towards the pins. After reading this, someone will post it on social media where it will soon become a meme and shared all over the world. Athletes are already in training to bring back gold and glory for curling/bowling. Conspiracies are fun that way. Sad but funny.

We used to idolize our astronauts. We had giant parades for them where everybody would litter the streets with paper, which, for some bizarre reason, was the greatest compliment one could have bestowed upon them. Giant confetti parades were a head-scratcher—literally. Thousands of pounds of paper fall on your head and your dandruff gets jealous and starts to itch. Someone should have had the cajones to toss out money instead and watch it become a thing. Now that would have been an event. It would have been a great supplemental income for the brave souls who sat on a giant exploding candle, praying that they would reach the atmosphere and return as something other than a patch of goo. But parades, while totally incomprehensible, made us all feel great as we did it together. You watched every second of the Macy's Thanksgiving Parade to see Santa Claus make his first appearance, announcing that Christmas shopping had arrived, and you better get your ass to Macy's or Gimbels or to the local junkyard, depending on your budget. That was followed by the Rose Bowl Parade, where the floats were made of flowers which should have launched a byzantine conspiracy, but never did. C'mon, CTers, stop being so lazy! They should have been having their own marches in the streets, ranting on about how Big Flora was bombarding our TV sets with not-so-subtle subliminal messages. Perhaps we should have combined the two weirdass ideas and tossed flowers onto the heads of our hero astronauts, and watched as it filled up their convertibles, and they would give us the queen wave, not out of politeness but to let us know that they were still breathing underneath all those flower petals. You'd think they would at least get a shoe deal or guest star on the latest sitcom. Nope. We littered. And maybe those damn conspiracy theorists are why that's an extinct tradition. Perhaps if they were truly committed to the notion that a massive event such as the moon landing was faked, their behavior wouldn't be so ass-backwards. They could have chosen to throw leaflets at the astronauts, telling them directly just how evil their participation in the fraudulent missions was. "You are part of the illusion that we landed and walked on the moon in an attempt to continue bilking the taxpayers out of billions of dollars, which you are using to take over the country as a secret, Jewish plot!" Ironically, the first, Jewish astronaut was actually the first astronaut, or cosmonaut—Yuri Gagarin, who never told anyone that he was Jewish for some, strange reason. The first, American Jewish astronaut was Judy Resnick who perished aboard *Challenger*—a perfect daily double in order to push a hare-brained conspiracy. But conspiracy theorists blew it for the rest

of us semi-sane people. Not only do we not celebrate our brave heroes anymore, but we actually denigrate all the men and women whose Stuff was so Right compared to our stuff, which wasn't even ranked. It would take another seventeen years before we thought enough of our astronauts to immortalize them, and they had to go up in a televised explosion, carrying an ordinary teacher before we would give a damn again. Perhaps it was the single, Jewish astronaut aboard that did it. And why didn't a conspiracy form that could allow us to believe that Christa McAuliffe was having tea with Elvis and Bigfoot and Marilyn and JFK? If you're going to undermine everything, give it a positive spin. Not every conspiracy needed to contribute to our self-loathing and hatred of all things government.

The concept that a bunch of lizard-brained conspiracy theorists were given the power to disparage actual mind-blowing achievements and the heroic men and women who performed them should be the real conspiracy—one worthy of a giant commission that will produce over one thousand pages that no one will read but everyone will insist that they know what it contains. Where is the second shuttle theory? Why hasn't anyone posted a meme about Hollywood SFX geniuses who were really the ones to create the unreal image of Challenger exploding, so we would be so heartbroken the spigot of money to NASA would never be shut off? From a singular, fiery explosion came such a period of national mourning we were shook out of our doldrums regarding an event that had become so pedestrian we stopped paying attention. We'd buy that. And then we could have pointed fingers at each other.

They blew it. And then we blew it.

Charlton Heston was right.

STUDIO 54

Studio 54 gets the Flying Fickle Middle Finger of Blame both coming and going. First, they were the leading figures in velvet rope snobbery as they only admitted the Beautiful People and the Most Glamorous Knobs in the World who were doing the types of things the rest of the Great Unwashed didn't dare to dream, even after reading The Best of *Penthouse* Forum Letters. Where else could you find a place that featured Divine doing blow off of child star Drew Barrymore's head as Mick Jagger, Timothy Leary, Jerry Hall, Liza Minelli, Halston, Jackie O, Debbie Harry, Al Pacino, and Bruce Jenner danced under the Giant Spoon while Salvador Dali and Bella Abzug made out on one of the sticky leather couches in the private corners? The level of debauchery that occurred within their hallowed halls would have made Caligula into a 12-step disciple. Studio 54 was the pipeline for every decadent and depraved Hollywood, music, and fashion A-lister where they could attempt to live up to the reputations they worked so hard to fake. They were through worrying about their public image or ending up in an embarrassing front-page story in the *National Enquirer*, or what remained of the gossip columnists, or the very least in a very special issue of *Highlights for Children* to give the kiddies an eyeful before their molars got drilled and filled with mercury poison at the dentist. No; they came loaded for bear as the jacked-up, clipboard security goons monitored the velvet ropes with a sniper's eye for the Fabulous and the anointed, whose breasts or sock-size, hidden in their pants, permitted entry. The wannabes and Also-rans were allowed in, based on their ability to be sycophants and give any of the A-listers a good time while slumming it with the penny-ante drug dealers. There were no publicists or political press attaches allowed in, so the hoi polloi could only drool and imagine the type of fun that the Ruling Class were afforded while they all clamored around Famous Ray's in the hopes of getting a slice of pizza, thus giving them weekend bragging rights at the water cooler on Monday for finding alternative entertainment. All the disappointed onlookers who didn't pass muster were left to dream their puerile fantasies of what it must be like to be pseudo-important, beautiful, and known. The Has-Beens also made Studio 54 their pilgrimage, hoping for one last shot at the spoils of fame—but all they could blurb out between their fifth tequila puff or snifter of Courvasaier was, "Excuse me. Do you know who I *used* to be?" If they were lucky, they might get a whiff of the carbon monoxide expelled by the limo tailpipe as Lauren Hutton, John Travolta, Grace Jones, Freddy Mercury, and Geraldo Rivera made their way, elbowing out all of the zeroes that cluttered the sidewalk and stood between the street and the opening to the Gates of Hell—someplace they all wanted to be but knew they never would. You had to blow a .33 blood alcohol level just to be allowed near the sidewalk, as sobriety was seriously frowned upon. Some of the more desperate hopefuls entertained hideous plans of macing the bouncers and ducking inside to hide at the feet of Paloma Picasso or Bette Midler, who would be too amused to turn them in. Plus, once inside, everyone appeared famous, even the likes of Lorna Luft who often had to show her ID to her fellow D-list celebrities—who were allowed in for sympathy's sake and to avoid their crying jags at the door. Studio 54 was the ultimate caste system which let New Yorkers know where they stood—if, for some reason, they never received their official memo or secret handshake instructions. And because what happened in New York definitely didn't stay in New York, the rest of the country, and the world, soon learned their social ranking thanks to the snobbish hellscape created by Steve Rubell

and Ian Schrager—two stiffs who would never have been allowed into
their own party had they not owned it to the financial backing of their
sugar daddy, Jack Dushey, whose last name was the perfect rhyme for
what he actually was.

So while the Dionysian club was local to the West Side, it helped
lower the self-esteem of the entire country. Page Six of the New York
Post had a way of filtering it down to the masses, who read with visions
of either rubbing elbows and doing poppers with the Best of the Best
or learning of their downfall for their indiscretions—or, just for having
the nerve to celebrate their addictions and depravity as the ultimate
thumb-on-nose to the rest of polite, boring society.

And they so deserve the middle finger for letting it all go to seed
and getting it closed up in 1980, just because Rubell and Schrager were
stupid enough to actually reveal that they made seven million in their
first year and out-earned everyone except the Mafia, which led the IRS

to sniff around and discover the who'd-a-thunk-it skimming of a mere 2.5 million. The only thing worse than hosting the world's best party to which we aren't invited was to get it all shut down so that we can't even entertain the notion of dreaming about it as futile wish fulfillment. They had the party, sent us the bill, and kept a bevy of lurid pictures just to remind us of all we missed. Jack Nicholson and Farrah Fawcett would have no problem finding another party, but where would the rest of us hang our foolish fantasies? Because after Studio 54 shuffled off this mortal coil, anyone else stupid enough to even think about having a brick-and-mortar bacchanal dismissed the idea and went back to a system where we could never learn where the party was, at least until Stefon would inform us of such underground establishments, as: *New York's hottest club is Spicy! This place has everything: sand worms, geishas, rock-eaters, a seven-level course in adult education, and, if you want to relax, you can kick back in your very own subway sleeping bag— which is that thing when you're on the train, and you sit between two guys in FUBU jackets.* We were back to our basement keggers or PG block parties, and the universe never seemed so glamorous and sinful again.

So screw you, Rubell and Schrager. You fucked us over trying to get in and then again as you did the frog-walk to jail. When a couple of mooks like you succeeded, we actually cheered—even though we weren't invited to the party.

And then you blew it.

It was pretty predictable.

You squashed our innocent souls just so you could feed the pretentious, and then you took away our zoo to ogle y'all in. As a result, we all suffer from a terminal identity crisis. The intersection between what we desire and our reality was pushed completely out of the realm of possibility. You deserved to have Mike Myers portray one of you.

AMERICAN MOTORS CORPORATION

Not to be confused with American Multi-Cinema—the gigantic multiplex movie theater chain now shitting the bed with virtually the entire movie distribution system—AMC was a link in the chain for blameapalooza due to its clusterfuck of a history, which is rife with so many twists and turns, it should be a limited show streaming on Hulu. Its sad little story began with the merger of Nash Kelvinator Corporation—which made the nifty Nash Rambler and Rebel—and the Hudson Motor Car Company—which produced some cool cars of their own, such as the Hudson Country Club Six Convertible and the Hudson Eight Convertible. They also tried to include Packard, which was no slouch in the automotive industry, but they had already merged with Studebaker without doing their due diligence and were grasping at any straws in the wind to survive. But a pissing contest between the Nash and Packard CEOs as to who would run the new company in a move destined to take on the Big Three scuttled that deal. So Nash and Packard did it without them, and the new company came to be American Motors Corporation, soon to be led by George Romney who would one day make an even bigger mistake by naming a son Willard Mitt.

From there, they went barreling onward down a slippery slope of misjudging what the public actually wanted. Long before it was necessary, AMC developed economy cars—so out went the Rambler and in came the Ambassador, which did goose sales a tad. But the much higher production costs meant they had slobberknockered their ability to secure working capital just to keep the sinking ship afloat. In the late 60s, they entered the muscle car field to compete with the Ford Mustang, Mercury Cougar, Pontiac GTO, and Trans Am, with their Javelin and AMX cars. And it would have worked, too, if it weren't for those meddling kids—specifically, the ones *not* buying Javelins and AMX cars. There are always some meddling kids. They are the perfect creatures on which to lay blame, especially when it involves their consumer tastes. But things were about to turn ugly at AMC. Really ugly.

AMC soon came out with the Gremlin, Matador, and Pacer. First, a note on the Gremlin: I bought one. I had been driving my stepmother's car before her ability to purchase much bigger and even uglier cars due to her marrying my dad, the Doctor (such as her banana yellow Montego). So, her 1967 Dodge Dart became mine when my dad bought her two dullard sons new cars. I could have bought a nicer car than the Gremlin, but I had already splurged on my first stereo system: a Nikko 2020 receiver, Sanyo turntable, and EPI 90 speakers, so that removed $500 from my total leaving me with $3200 left to spend on my first, new automobile in 1976.

There were three cars in my price range: a Dodge Dart (again), a Plymouth Volare, or the AMC Gremlin. The Dart was right out, as no kid wants to buy a repeat of the model that had been passed down from their wicked stepmother. The Volare seemed like something your grandmother would drive and then regret immediately. So that left the Gremlin, which did come in a sport pack—which basically entailed having a white racing stripe painted down the side. Cool.

The Gremlin was a six-cylinder ensconced in aluminum foil. It was a rear-wheel drive with all the weight in the front and absolutely no ballast in the back end. This meant two things: first, it drove like a bat out of hell, but if an ant farted on the side of the road, the wind blast would cause you to involuntarily change lanes. And if there was any moisture on the roads, you had to load up the hatchback with cement blocks to add enough traction to even move. If the forecast called for a light snow flurry, you were taking the bus. And only double-leg amputees and dwarves could actually sit in the back seat. Grumpy, Sneezy, and Dopey would always be left to take the bus, especially if Snow White was in the mood to pick up hitchhikers.

The Pacer was known as the *pregnant egg*, as it's raison d'être was to be a small, economy car with a wide base for more interior room and superior traction. The Pacer was also the second American car to have rack-and-pinion steering, behind the Ford Pinto. You can see where this is going.

The Pacer, although hailed by most of the automobile consumer magazines, failed to impress the marketplace. Thus, it's been relegated to the dustbin of history with its cameos in *Wayne's World* and *Wayne's World II*. Mike Myers, again.

The Matador was AMC's full-size family car, whose marketing campaign was, "What's a Matador?"

Exactly.

No matter how many times they restyled it, it just didn't move—sales-wise, not actually move-wise. Finally, they found its niche as a law enforcement vehicle and TV cop show car. It even made it into James Bond's *Man with a Golden Gun*. That alone should have pushed it into the stratosphere, but as life is often 90 percent timing, 10 percent lighting, they missed their window—the combo of the oil crisis and double-digit inflation killed it and Toyota; Nissan (Datsun) and Honda basically took over the American automobile market. Rumor had it that the Japanese automakers paid Hervé Villechaize to be seen driving a Matador to ensure continued tanking sales.

And that's where things have stood for decades. The US was once the proud maker of the finest vehicles on the road, the envy of people all over the globe. Our Cadillacs were mighty symbols of opulence, wealth, and the vehicle of choice for Mafia bosses, doctors, and lawyers who preferred their *Jew Canoes* to stand out, even if it meant parallel parking would be a bitch. The classic finned or muscle cars of the 50s such as the T-bird, Corvette, or even the Little Deuce Coupe were the dreams of winsome teenagers. The posters adorned their bedroom walls, and their calendars were found in many a dad's garage, but for slightly different reasons. But those days are long gone. Over the years, we were so desperate for something that wouldn't break the bank we even bought a car from freaking Yugoslavia, a country that doesn't even exist anymore. Now, we're all in Toyota Camrys and RAV4s, Subaru Outbacks and Honda Civics. Jesus, I even drive a car from South Korea with a Hispanic-sounding name: the Kia Seltos. How fucked up is that? The Big Three are still rolling along, but most of their cars are assembled in Mexico. So even our American-made cars celebrate Cinco de Mayo!

Nobody writes about American cars anymore—not The Beach Boys, not Springsteen, and not even country artists who used to wax poetic about their Ford Trucks. Now they and their hip hop brethren can be seen riding in stretch limos, probably built by Peugeot or Fiat—which, embarrassingly enough, owns Chrysler. Blame that gaff on one of their own, Lee Iacocca. So I give shit-ton of blame to AMC for

vomiting up a load of crappy cars during a time when we really needed something a whole lot better. Excuse me while I see if my Korean/Mexican subcompact hybrid is charged up via my neighbor's exterior house plug. And don't blame me if your utility bill skyrockets. By leaving your outlets unmonitored, you blew it.

ATMs

America's first automatic teller machine (ATM) had its public coming-out party on September 2, 1969, and we've been playing it like a casino—screwing us over with house money—ever since. It first amazed us by dispensing cash to customers at Chemical Bank in Rockville Centre, New York. The customer inserted a card and hit a bunch of number options, and thus "spin the wheel, make the deal" operated on virtually every corner. And we have never recovered.

Long before most people passed out from drinking at the bar, we ran out of money. The ATM solved that little problem. You didn't have to anticipate your financial needs before the weekend started, which meant actually going to the bank during your lunch break on Fridays and standing in line along with every other asshole who anticipated a weekend of debauchery—or at least a decent meal that wasn't at Taco Bell. Don Wetzel invented automatic baggage-handling equipment, a system that allowed our baggage to be misrouted at warp speed— but he also developed the ATM, for which he deserves a swift kick in the yarbles. Besides the increased number of alcoholics it created (an increase of 10.3 percent in the 70s), the ATM also created the first form of hacking as criminals devised all sorts of clever ways to get our PINs—which was another thing, we had to create and memorize a PIN. This was the introduction to the wonderful world of passwords, and just how much did that little mnemonic pissery ruin our lives? Plus, another ridiculous event joined our lexicon to stand side-by-side with "the dog ate my homework," which was, "the ATM ate my debit card," or, "what do you mean I have negative nine dollars in my account?!"

The ATM actually wasn't universally accepted right away. It seemed that people were used to standing in line at the bank, and the term "banker's hours" actually meant something then. Banks often had strange hours of operation, such as open from 9:53 a.m. to 10:48 a.m. on alternating Mondays, Wednesdays, and Fridays—except on leap years, when they closed five minutes earlier to make up for having to be open that extra day. So, actually finding a time when you could go to the bank produced inventive excuses to take off from work. Teller lines were like Disneyland rides as they wound themselves throughout the lobby until you didn't know which way you were facing anymore. When you finally reached the Holy Grail of the teller herself, you encountered the Moment of Judgement where you would be vulnerable to ridicule should your checking and savings account contain just enough money to purchase a Nestle's Crunch Bar—and that was only if the candy store had a layaway plan. But still, they were human... sort of, and you didn't have to memorize PIN numbers or even your account number. Just pass them your bank book and they would scribble the day's transaction with handwriting that made your doctor's prescriptions seem like wedding-invitation cursive. But at least you felt safe—until the hottest day of the year in mid-August when two men wearing overcoats and ski masks skipped their way into the bank. The first ATMs were positioned in dark and lonely corners of the landscape and questionable characters hovered about, waiting for your withdrawal and exit into the closest back alley. Somebody was going to have a great weekend, but it sure as hell wasn't going to be you.

And balancing your checkbook became impossible, as too many of the visits were made in the middle of the night where a round of drinks with friends quickly converted into a bender and you had no idea where you put the slip with the transaction on it, as it wasn't in your wallet or purse—which would have made the most sense, but not after eight strawberry margaritas with a kamikaze chaser after each

one. And it might not have been the same as the look of disappoint-
ment when the teller notified you of insufficient funds, but somehow,
having an infernal machine tell you the same news was even more mor-
tifying. You knew the teller wasn't making big bucks either, but the
ATM was cold and uncaring. Well, so was the teller, but her ill-fitting
clothes at least telegraphed her financial plight to you.

Now let's discuss the ATM fee. The fee is how most companies,
especially banks, kill you. Just look at your cable and mobile phone
bill and you realize that they have a license to print money, but the
ATM fee was the one that caused our teeth to grind in the middle of
the night. What, if anything, was more patently absurd and annoying
than paying money to get our money? If ATM deployers had a dollar
for every time someone moaned about ATM fees, they could all go to
Aruba for a month and let cardholders rediscover the joy of queuing at
the teller window during bank hours to cash a check. And then there
was the increased fee for going to an ATM from another bank, because
you chose the bank that had no ATMs anywhere near the places you
frequent—like bars, bowling alleys, and that ex-girlfriend you like
to stalk. So they charged you for the service of one computer system
talking to another. Did they have their own union? Just where was the
cost to any bank for having this universal banking system that they
were all tied into to deduct money from *your* bank but dispensed by
the machine from *their* bank? The fact that the deduction was instan-
taneous told us that it wasn't taxing their computer at all. If it took
a few minutes while it was *thinking*, maybe we could all understand
and accept it. If the little blue, spinning circle appeared—as it does a
thousand times a day on your laptop—you would be angry, but at least
you would get it. Banks are swine, and the ATM is just a mechanized
version of their swinery.

We should have ignored the brutish machines when they began dot-
ting the landscape in the 70s. We should have firmly held onto our habit
of taking our valuable time off work to make the pilgrimage to the bank
to wait our turn to see the stone-faced teller either hand over the crisp,
new bills or deny our request with a totally non-sympathetic, "I'm sorry."

We have lost, in so many ways, our ability to show our fellow travelers our anger in the moments we need to the most. We can't slam the receiver down on the phone and we can't threaten to take our piddly dollars to another bank and storm out in a huff. Those days are long gone. So, let's hear it for the ATM: six degrees of separation to the selfie. Now that's the definition of blowing it.

SATURDAY NIGHT LIVE

We had never seen anything like *Saturday Night Live* when it premiered in the autumn of 1975. And not knowing what to expect means that you aren't invested in its success or failure. You might be pleasantly surprised or just think it annoying and not worth another viewing. So the major problem was that the original Not Ready for Prime Time Players raised expectations so high, that it's been totally unreasonable to expect them to be met on a consistent basis, let alone for the 40-plus years it's been on. And because of their novel approach to comedy, they were anything but risk-averse, and the same was true of their musical guests. I had never heard of Devo until the night they were the musical talent and I witnessed Mark Mothersbaugh struggling to get out of his orange jumper as the band played their bizarre cover of the Rolling Stones's *Satisfaction (I Can't Get No)*. Of course, it helped that I was a freshman in college and at 11:30 p.m. every Saturday night, it would be a reasonable assumption that I must have already gone through several hits of my Michigan Mask Bong, meaning I would have guffawed at "no smoking" PSAs. Point taken. But the problem was that, as Hunter Thompson so eloquently put it, we bought the ticket, so we took the ride. But for six decades? The restaurant that vacillates between culinary orgasm to blowing chunks in the back-alley dumpster eventually loses our business. Or should. There would be no excuse for returning. There were only so many brilliant comedians and comedy writers that landed the gig simultaneously that brought us must-see TV. And just as a broken clock is correct twice a day, even the nadir years brought us incredible talent, such as Eddie Murphy, Billy Crystal, and Chris Farley. But was it worth it to suffer through Victoria Jackson, Horatio Sanz, or Gail Matthius? You can count on TV reviewer headlines to read *Saturday Night Dead* at least once every third year. The genius talents such as Kristen Wiig, Bill Hader, and Kate McKinnon probably would have broken through anyway, such was the abundance and flexibility of their abilities. And the guest hosts also became tiresome, as it was just a parade of the latest *it* person from the entertainment biz letting us know how much of a childhood dream had just been fulfilled by their initial hosting duties, far outstripping the gazillion dollars they had made from their last film/TV show/album/sports championship.

NBC has canceled much better shows after a limited run without thinking twice. It was often the equivalent of a movie opening on a Friday and transitioning into an in-flight movie that same night. Multiple times during the run, NBC should have had a number of famed vaudeville hooks yank the cast offstage as they were waving goodbyes at the end of the show, while the band played *Thank God and Greyhound You're Gone.* Or close with a two-hour, "very special" movie and bring back all the cast members to reminisce their catchphrases, ala *Seinfeld,* and then we can all criticize the shit out of it and just see what else was on. Because there was always something else on. Most of it was shite, but TV has always just been a time filler for shut-ins or people with serious relationship problems.

And while we're at it, cancel *60 Minutes,* too. The irony of that show is that the "tick...tick...tick..." that opens the show now sounds like the time bomb that we all secretly hope actually goes off. It just lost something now that we don't have Mike Wallace ambushing the director of some clinic that does in vitro fertilizations with pigmen. We have cell phones to do that, and Project Veritas for comic, ambush relief. The best photojournalism comes from teens shooting video selfies when they stumble onto mega stories, such as George Floyd

getting murdered in the street by racist cops. They were smart not to continue segments such as *Point/Counterpoint*, as what was the point when the original SNL did it better, anyway? It never mattered what they were blathering on about, as long as the "Jane, you ignorant slut" was uttered, and then you could see turn to the late-night movie of *Gidget Gets a Rash*. And who in their right mind would or could replicate Andy Rooney's "Haven't You Ever Wondered" segment? There will probably be some journalist curmudgeon that could approximate Andy's whining, but who would want that gig—to air out all of his grievances in front of an audience that couldn't give a shit, other than "Drunk Uncle," and that was already done. We have all found our little niche sources for news that allows us to nod our little heads in agreement and shout "YES!" at the television when they make our points for us. Perhaps a final episode, where *60 Minutes* investigates itself, finds itself rife with corruption, and then the show and the run suddenly ends without warning. Round up the usual suspects. Anderson Cooper, we're talking to you.

Kaboom, motherfuckers!

NOT EVERYTHING IS SMALL STUFF

In 1973, Clive Sinclair introduced a series of pocket calculators that changed the industry, making calculators small and light enough to fit in your pocket, giving bullies just one more reason to take your lunch money when you pulled out your calculator at the bus stop to determine just how much the ride was costing you per mile. It wasn't as obvious as the pocket protector, with a shit-ton of pens sticking out. But it was close. They were not only much smaller and thinner than their competitors, but also much cheaper, making their advanced technology available to the masses. School kids would never again understand math or how to make change on their own again.

In 1973, State Rep. Jim Kaster introduced a bill in the Texas legislature that would have required criminals to give their victims twenty-four hours' notice before they committed a crime, unless you canceled your being a victim before that, in which case the twenty-four hour cancellation fee was waived. The notice could be either oral or in writing, or you could have used semaphores or even smoke signals to your intended victim, but then you would need to state "the nature of the crime to be committed and the time and place it is to be committed" or "it wouldn't be considered a legal crime." Kaster, showing all of the logic of a televangelist on meth, argued: "Obviously the criminal is not going to do it, but this would be another punishment that could be added to the penalty." The bill was defeated, probably because of legislature members not wanting to appear soft on crime, or hard on criminal time management—whichever floated their collective boats. But it foreshadowed just how wackadoo Texas politics would become.

September 1974: Marlene McCauley spoke at the National Pretzel Convention on the theme of *Pretzels in a Changing World,* as she was so disturbed by Steely Dan's 1974 album, *Pretzel Logic,* that she was all in a twist. McCauley was founder of the Pretzels for God movement—which she might have stolen from *Agnes of God,* but that film didn't premier until eleven years later. Perhaps Marlene was a clairvoyant but just didn't know it, due to her weird pretzel fetish. Her stated goal for the movement was to restore the pretzel to its former place in Christian worship, which was just her way of justifying her deep love for Pabst Blue Ribbon. She had the epiphany that the pretzel had been invented by Christians in the fifth century to eat during Lent because there was only so much mutton a good Christian would eat. Its shape symbolized arms crossed in prayer or a fat guy with his arms folded—depending on just how much Pabst you had that night. But in the modern world, it became the butt of jokes in not one, but two *Seinfeld* episodes: one where Kramer had to say a line about pretzels in a Woody Allen movie, and another where George was hawking a brand of which he was their paid spokesman, and the producers allowed it if they got a piece of the action.

She said, "The little pretzel does have a joyful feeling about it, and that's a wonderful thing in these troubled times." Separation of Church and Plate.

Philadelphia Eagles all-pro linebacker Tim Rossovich showed the public he was so tough that he could eat glass from beer mugs. Then, a Harvard student wanted to prove that Rossovich wasn't that special, so he, too, ate a lightbulb. And what do you know, the fad caught on among university students. It was basically the Tide Pod Challenge of the 1970s. Obviously, authorities had to step in.

Obviously.

Calculators, advanced warning for criminal activity, pretzels, light bulb munching, Tide Pods—individually, just some small glitches in *The Matrix*. Together, with a host of other lighter fare—too small to make *Ripley's Believe It Or Not,* but just right to insert into the thesis of how even small stuff indicates how we're blowing it—the little lemmings march in time proving that nothing is too small to be weird.

THE OPENING OF DISNEYWORLD AND EPCOT CENTER

Before the Mouse invaded mid-Florida, Miami Beach was the Mecca for Northeast, Jewish snowbirds to travel to every Christmas/ Chanukah season. Eastern and Northeast Yellowbird Airlines ferried a non-stop parade of doctors, dentists, lawyers, and the other great Jewish stereotypes, with their brood in tow to feast on gefilte fish roasting under a blazing, tropical sun. The concept of Miami Beach had become ingrained in the psyche of an entire generation. Its name was a metaphor for sunny days, sexy nights, and abstract aspirations of the good life that lingered just beyond reach. The Rat Pack—Jacki Gleason, Johnny Desmond, and a bevy of A-list strippers (known then as peelers)—performed in the top hotels, such as The Fontainebleau Hotel, The Di Lido, The Cadillac, and The Americana.

This was where my family vacationed in the late 60s and early 70s. We would alternate hotels each year, staying at The Fontainebleau, The Americana, or the Doral, arriving at our destination in a rented Cadillac to join the procession of Caddys, Lincoln Continentals, and—for the Jew without Germanyphobia—a Mercedes Benz. The palm trees were lit up with floodlights of pastel greens and reds, while the hotels were bathed in aqua and the other colors of the art deco era, giving my sister and me our first acid flash-forwards. Inside, there would be huge columns lit up like giant pearls, and the lobby had shades of purple back- and front-lighting the massive front desk. At night, the entire facade of the hotels were a bright purple that reflected in their cur-vaceous swimming pools, so your senses were under constant assault from a monolithic rainbow. These were grand palaces that catered to the nouveau and wannabe ruling class, and the kids were brought along to glimpse their future of conspicuous consumption, duode-nal ulcers, and eventual divorces—preceded by the choosing of your favorite parent who never actually liked you. But from our innocent viewpoint, we were being invited into the world of adults, and the rite of passage had as much social status as the time you were finally allowed to stay up and watch *Johnny Carson*. You didn't know the guests or understand most of what they were saying, but you knew it was titillating and probably sexual in ways you couldn't understand but you laughed anyway, pretending to get the joke, because one day, you *would* get the joke.

The fundamental tedium was the enduring reality of these vaca-tions. It was part of the ritual. There actually wasn't a whole lot to do, especially for the sub-teenage set. During the day, there was the beach or the pool, and if your parents played golf (mine didn't) and one of the siblings were old enough, you could be left to your own devices in the day hours—which, for my sister and me, was mostly devoted to walking along the boulevard to the Castaways Hotel. The restaurant/lounge looked a lot like the Polynesian restaurants in Boston's China-town, which lured us in with their grand interiors and rattan furniture only to let us down with incredibly subpar food. But we kept return-ing, for such was our lot. It was always about appearances.

Dinnertime was a formal affair at any of the multitude of hotel restaurants, where we were forced to dress up as little gents and ladies and eat filet mignon and other entrees we were typically denied at our local eateries (by parents who insisted we order off the kiddie menu until our bar mitzvahs—and sometimes, well into our twenties). Our parents would be free to drink, which meant Chivas on the rocks for Dad and Cuba Libres for Mom, and keep them coming. It was perhaps the most surreal moments, during these trips, to watch them slowly get buzzed in preparation for their pre-planned sex later that evening, followed by falling asleep in front of the television—which pretty much summed up their home life, if you removed the sex. But that dystopian reverie was not to last. Besides the financial underpinnings that crushed the life out of the Miami Beach life of the 40s, 50s, and 60s, the invasion of Orlando provided the final death knell for the northeast snowbirds looking to escape the cold and to also shut the flapping gums of their children who were drawn to Orlando like pigs to slop. If Miami Beach of yesteryear was a polished sentence, Orlando was a non sequitur.

In 1870, Miami Beach was a glorified sand trap that could have been home on any of the multitude of golf courses that would soon be built. It was also an overgrown mangrove ridge, as that lovely vegetation mostly grows in brackish water—the type of beach that you don't even dip your toes in. New Jersey residents Henry Lum and his son, Charles, decided to change all that by combing their couch cushions, as the swamp sold for the low, low price of 25 cents an acre. They tried to turn it into a coconut farm, but they couldn't get the tune "you put the lime in the coconut" out of their heads, even though it wouldn't be written for over one hundred years. It was a moot point, as either rats or rabbits ate the coconuts (as they were sick of the song, too—and rumor had it that it was they who came up with the nickname, *Nilsson Schmillson)*. But the father/son team shit the bed regarding being very good Floridians, as their two seven-irons-in-a-golf-bag legs just didn't look right in swim trunks. Eventually, some putz named John S. Collins bought the area and actually figured out how to grow things of value, but his real claim to fame was getting Miami's main road named after him, so he's the guy to curse when you're stuck in horrible traffic. By 1915, the town would officially be incorporated, and Collins partnered with Carl Fisher and the banking Lummus brothers to turn the beach into an honest hunk of land, perfect for hordes of dishonest people to make scads of money and, eventually, get the TV show *Miami Vice* made, which caused major fashion trends that Collins, Fisher, and the Lummus brothers would be turning over in their graves had they known what *schmata* they would one day be responsible for...sort of.

Much of South Florida was built on drained swampland, although Donald Trump's residence in Mar-a-Lago at least supports the notion that the swampland wasn't so much "drained" as "relocated." But compared to the creation of Miami Beach, that was relatively easy. In Miami Beach, laborers had to clear out the mangroves, deepen the channels of water around it, and fill in the area with actual soil to create honest-to-God land. Their adding alligators, boa constrictors, and mosquitos the size of Buicks was, as the laborers would say, "just one, big joke on tourists."

When Walt Disney World opened in 1971, Orlando began its transformation to "The Theme Park Capital of the World." Orlando was named after Orlando Reeves, a soldier killed by Seminole Indians—because nothing says, "Hey, come visit our beautiful, tourist trap" than a murder that just might have been deserved. The US Army built Fort Gatlin southeast of present-day downtown Orlando to protect settlers from the Indians, but just ask Mr. Reeves how that went. By 1840, a small settlement known as Jernigan was founded, named after Aaron Jernigan—allegedly, the first settler to come to the area renamed it Orlando, as Jernigan drove cattle down from Jacksonville, and who wants a Florida town named after a guy who screams the Wild West? By 1850, Jernigan had a post office and a combination laundromat and liquor store, and by 1856, the community had bulged northward and changed its name to Orlando—but the date of the first gift shop remains a mystery.

And finally, the man, the myth, the legend, Walt Disney, put his personal stamp on the area in the most American way possible: pure fraud. Walt created multiple fake companies (with adorable names such as M.T. Lott Real Estate) to buy Florida land in the 1960s. This let him acquire what is now Disney World while avoiding suspicion, although many thought that the mustache was a pretty poor disguise. The stores on the Magic Kingdom's Main Street, U.S.A. shop windows are the names of those original companies, which was just another way of Walt putting thumb on nose and giving all of us the raspberry— especially local and federal law enforcement.

In came the hotels, such as Holiday Inn, Hyatt, Marriott, and Sheraton—the fast food of the hospitality industry. Disney would, of course, supplement those with their own Magic Kingdom-styled hotels. While the Miami Beach hotels had furniture that were more "art and artifice" with no practical use for the human body, the Orlando hotels were utilitarian and nondescript. They wanted anything special to be contained within the theme parks. The opening of Disneyworld in 1971 meant that families such as mine would never make the trek out to California, which was why Walt built up Central Florida in the first place: we weren't heading west in the first place. I had grown up watching *The Magical World of Disney,* but had never fantasized about going to a theme park where the show and its characters came to life. I also had never been an amusement park enthusiast, as roller coasters frightened the bejesus out of me—but my dad, having lost the guidance of our mother years back, was ignorant of those facts, so we made the dutiful trek to Orlando. Hunter Thompson once wrote, "Life should not be a journey to the grave with the intention of arriving safely in a pretty and well-preserved body, but rather to skid in broadside in a cloud of smoke, thoroughly used up, totally worn out, and loudly proclaiming 'Wow! What a Ride!'" That could be a fair description of visiting Disney World, except it didn't count for the lines. The ability to enjoy the thrills of Space Mountain, or the Buñuel-like weirdness of Mr. Toad's Wild Ride—assuming one has a proclivity for such things—paled after the line's wait eclipsed the length of the ride by a factor of ten. Or maybe twenty. Better break out the pocket calculator.

The Disney characters that roamed the park and stalked the visitors in silence gave more than nuance to the word "creepy." The Park reeked of paranoia, and it was fitting that all who have met their demise within the not-so-cozy confines of Disney World had their carcasses dragged off the premises so the place of death couldn't be fingered to Walt & Company—because any child with a potential mutant gene for heart disease will have surely discovered their first symptom (and possibly their last) at Disney World. The Park was famous for giving VIP tours to the expats of Studio 54 so they could enjoy the perks and privileges the rest of us couldn't even dream about, one more time.

The Disney theme parks were the inverse of the Miami Beach experience. Instead of the parents bringing their children to have a brief peek of the life of adulthood, this was the kids dragging their parents—literally, kicking and screaming—into the perverse universe of what Walt believed children wanted and needed: an expensive trip through Disney-copyrighted material to permanently imprint their brand on both the young minds and the decaying ones while they still had the money and stamina to partake. As the Disney film-and-television empire grew, so did the branding. Buy the ticket, take the ride— brought to you by *Toy Story*.

EPCOT was originally an acronym for Experimental Prototype Community of Tomorrow, a utopian city with all the George Orwell and H.G. Wells underpinnings that word invokes. Its original idea was to create a city that would emerge from the creative centers of American industry and, if that didn't shake you to your core, you weren't well read, well lived, or both. In future shock terms, Epcot was to be a testing lab where all the residents were ignorant guinea pigs to the whims and *Sturm und Drang* of corporate America. The positive take of that notion was that you got to sample New Coke before they foisted the swill onto an unsuspecting public.

Walt's death put a halt on that concept, as the Keepers of the Flame decided that without Walt himself acting as Mayor, no one wanted to have any possible liability for the ensuing lawsuits that were sure to come. Their indecision on what to do with Frankenstein's Monster was such that they decided to create a mishmash of the two central themes—the cutting edge of technology, and an international showcase of customs and cultures. So at least you might be able to sample your first Belgian waffle while wondering where the fuck you were and why you were there in the first place. When the park opened in 1982, they installed a plaque at the opening which read: "To all who come to this place of joy, hope and friendship, welcome."

Epcot was inspired by Walt Disney's creative vision—or, possibly, his love of magic mushrooms. Here, human achievements were celebrated through imagination, wonders of enterprise, and concepts of a future that promised new and exciting benefits for all—or at least a very expensive place to have a very expensive nosh.

Epcot was basically the smart kid, overdosing on Adderall and thinking that every cockamamie idea he or she had should be designed and implemented, no matter how insane it might be—and if you can make a buck on it by attracting the rubes from all over the world, so much the better. After all, they didn't come up with the motto, "there's

a sucker born every minute," but they certainly refined the concept. And if it got us out of single-digit temperatures and shoveling the 12 inches in 12 hours of snow now obstructing the front door and driveway, then hallelujah.

The Miami Beach hotels had no such plaque in their lobbies that Epcot did—the whole, "Entertain, inform, inspire," yadda yadda yadda. But they did have a gaggle of people more than willing to point out the closest place you could get a drink, regardless of the year of your birth.

EPCOT's compromise to the kiddies was *Futureworld* which featured all kinds of avant-garde pavilions such as a geodesic sphere and, of course, rides, many of which were simulated, which actually brought up the stomach bile faster than the first plunged-into-darkness drop at *Space Mountain.* There was a lot about space, energy, automobiles, communication, and the sea and life on Earth, so your vacation could actually be counted as extra credit for school as you were forced to learn stuff, and your parents would write it all off their taxes as school supplies. The World Showcase allowed you to do the, *If It's Tuesday It Must Be Belgium* tour, with various countries' pavilions scattered around a man-made lagoon of brackish water fit to fill the canal of *It's a Small World.* The upside was that the restaurants in the pavilions sold alcoholic beverages pertaining to the country of origin, so Mom and Dad could get snockered while convincing themselves about the worldliness they were exposing their kids to. And when they passed out on one of the ubiquitous benches lining the paths, you were free to go perform wonderful feats of mischief undetected by the Disney Gestapo.

Disney didn't really kill Miami Beach. The Beach was in its death rattle long before Disney World—and certainly before Epcot opened. The art deco feel of Miami Beach traveled a little bit northward to South Beach, which became much more trendy. The former Studio 54 crowd, along with the most pretentious professional athletes of the day, would hang out in designer Speedos and dental-floss bikinis, revealing their perfect bodies and, once again, making the rest of us feel like part of a leper colony just happy to sometimes get close enough to radiate in their brilliance, the star-fucker-star-fucker-star.

But spoofs were made of the Disney experience, such as *Wally World*, while real films and period pieces showcased the real cool that was Miami Beach, such as *Scarface*, *The Flamingo Kid,* and parts of *Godfather II*. Miami Beach was Miles Davis while Disney World and Epcot were Kenny G. Either way, Florida died decades ago. Time to chop up the body and mail it all over the country—especially before they blow another election.

MATTHEW BRODERICK

WarGames came out in 1983 and it starred Matthew Broderick as the movies' first depiction of computer hacking. And what a horrible message it sent. Instead of people coming away with the hair-raising thought that those idiots really could blow up the world, instead, they saw how cool he was, inspiring copycat behavior. The little pisher even got himself a hot girlfriend in the process, as he saved the world from the bullshit *he* fucking caused in the first place. As a result, we all learned just how hapless and unqualified our Department of Defense was at keeping the world safe from having a giant oopsie. They should have had Eddie Deezen's computer geek, Malvin, as the star. He was high up on the autism spectrum and inspired one of the great ad libs of all time when Maury Chaykin shouted, "Mr. Potato Head!" repeatedly at him for revealing his total lack of social skills. The film would have been hilarious and wouldn't have inspired people to see hacking as a noble pastime and possibly even a profession. In the GRU, it's considered a training manual. Gen Xrs who saw the film morphed into the people currently hacking into my Facebook account and sending me a link on Instant Messenger asking me if it's really me in the video, just so I click on it and watch as some Pac Man-like virus gobbles up my hard drive and all my files I was too stupid not to save on the cloud or a thumb drive or some other weirdly named nonsense. And his best friend in *Ferris Bueller's Day Off*, Cameron Frye—man, did he get thrown under the bus (or the Ferrari). Sure, he claimed that it was the "best day of his life" and that he'll be OK after he and Morris "have a little chat." But from what we knew of Morris, Cameron was in for much more than a chat. He was most likely beaten to a bloody pulp and tossed out on his ass where he wound up homeless, sleeping on a bench in front of the Chicago Institute of Art and dreaming of George Seurat's *A Sunday Afternoon on the Island of La Grande Jatte*. Or he ended up back at the bottom of the pool, this time with a large rock tied to his ankles. Life moves pretty fast, but if you didn't have the cajones to stand up to a jerkwad like Ferris Bueller from taking your dad's restored Ferrari and crashing through the giant garage picture window, then you deserved to be eating lead paint chips for dinner inside a refrigerator box under some bridge near the Chicago Loop.

So after his initial, horrible example from *WarGames*, Broderick got fucking promoted to uber cool dude in *Ferris Bueller's Day Off*. There used to be no mistaking who the cool guy was in the film. It was

James Dean, Elvis (*Jailhouse Rock* Elvis, not "dying while taking a shit with a heart full of drugs and peanut butter and bananas" Elvis), Steve McQueen, Charles Bronson, Paul Newman, and even some of the Brat Pack like Emilio Estevez, Rob Lowe—hell, even Judd Nelson, whose quote from *The Breakfast Club*, "You're a neo-maxi-zoom-dweebie" so applied to Bueller. But he was a self-indulgent dickwad, who was adored by the hot girl and won over his psychotic sister in the end. If any of us tried imitating that in school, the real cool kids would have thumped us in the stairwell or playground, or in the Goddamned class-room watched over by the clueless substitute teacher who just wanted to survive the day and collect the laughable paycheck. Elevating that dillhole to cool status is still reverberating today, dammit! Have you been to Starbucks?

Broderick almost gets a pass for playing closer to the nebbish bone in later roles, such as Leopold Bloom in Broadway's version of *The Pro-ducers* and as a high school teacher who despises his uber-motivated student, Tracey Flick, in *Election*. But the damage had already been done. Until he does a televangelist, eyeball-leaking mea culpa to atone for his earlier sins, he still makes the list about how things actually got blown. Someone should have given him a wedgie as he was collecting either of his Tony Awards. And if Oscar comes calling, it would be time to go all thermonuclear war on his ass.

THE OZONE LAYER

A long time ago, in a galaxy not so far away, we were told that there was a hole developing in the ozone layer. Of course, we had questions. What's ozone? Why is it in a layer, and what the hell does that have to do with my spray deodorant? Scientists had succinct and clear answers: "Ozone," they explained, "is a colorless gas with powerful oxidizing properties. It is formed from oxygen by electrical discharges or ultraviolet light."

"Interesting. So what does a layer of this stuff do?"

"Basically, it acts like sunscreen."

"Ah," we said. "So without it...?"

"We cook like ants under a magnifying glass."

This was easy to digest. Way too many of us knew what cooking ants under a magnifying glass was like, although none of us will admit it *now*. And of course, now *we're* the ants.

"So tell us more? How do we fix this?"

"Human activities effectively punched a hole in it, through the use of gasses like chlorofluorocarbons (CFCs) in spray cans and refrigerants, which break down ozone molecules in the upper atmosphere."

"Ah, I'm beginning to get a bead on this. So what products contain CFCs?"

"Aerosol sprays, such as hair spray, deodorant, cleaning solvents, fast-food cartons, old refrigerators, and fire extinguishers."

"So if we stop using that stuff, will the ozone layer repair itself?"
"Basically."

And that was that. Now, it wasn't all that simple. Getting women to stop using Aqua Net in the 80s to keep their towers of hair in place was no easy feat. Good thing hair styles are trends that come and go, so the problem fixed itself. We replaced CFCs with hydrofluorocarbons (HFCs), replaced our old refrigerators and air conditioners, started using roll-ons, and watched Styrofoam become a flash point for recycling.

Years later, the drumbeat for Global Warming or Climate Change or Global Climate Warming Change sounded and we were told we were all doomed unless we changed a buttload of things, mostly getting off fossil fuels. Now that was confusing. First, we were often given doomsday scenarios that never happened, so the climatologists became akin to the religious nutjobs who were always predicting the end of the world by a certain date and, when the date came and went, they actually had the balls to say they were right and that we just misinterpreted exactly what they meant—and then we were given a new date. So we just laughed at them (well, most of us did) and paid them no mind. Until they became Seventh Day Adventists.

So there were many problems with climate doomsday predictions and their fixes. Americans love fossil fuels, or at least we simply adhere to the motto, "go with what you know." We were amused by the fact that they were formed when gigantic creatures called dinosaurs all died and their bodies decomposed into bubbling masses of black goo that could power our cars and heat our homes. That's just too damn funny to give up. Plus, a lot of our entertainment was based on the stuff. We had James Dean as Jett, covered in crude in the film *Giant*. Jed Clampett missed a squirrel or something and accidentally stumbled onto Black Gold and lived the life in Beverly Hills with a snooty banker sniveling at his feet while Elly May cavorted in a swimsuit around the cee-ment pond. Our entire lives revolved around Texas Tea, and you can't be asking some tough, rough-neck to start driving a hybrid Prius that runs quieter than a ninja warrior. Hell, we used to poke holes in our mufflers just to intensify the throaty, muscular sound of a car in motion so everybody knew that Eli was coming, hide your hearts and cover your ears.

Plus, we're told that climate change causes *everything* bad. Summer is boiling hot, that's climate change. But so are the freezing cold winters. The increase in hurricanes, tornados, blizzards, frogs, locusts, and slaying of the first born have all been attributed to climate change. We don't like having a cornucopia of problems to deal with, as just one, medium-sized challenge freaked us out. When you took your car in to the mechanic and he told you that your carburetor was on the fritz, the alternator wasn't alternating, your belts all needed tightening, and you threw a rod and your staff no longer comforts you, you told him to pound sand and to pick the one thing to fix that will make sure the engine doesn't blow up, because we can live through everything else. Often that meant disabling the check engine light. It's the same thing when we visited the doctor. She couldn't really locate the problem, so she told you it was lupus. Your body hated itself and was attacking itself mercilessly, which forced you to wear a sombrero so wide it had its own zip code as you couldn't be out in the sun, ever—and that butterfly rash on your face, and the aches in your joints that sound like the screen door on Granny's house back in the day? Yup, it was all from lupus. But when you ask if they could confirm the diagnosis, they shrug their shoulders and tell you that they can confirm what it's *not*, but that's all. When you pressed them on it, they admitted it wasn't actually lupus, but lupus fit, so they suggested everyone pretend it was lupus. Otherwise, it had to be cancer. That meant you were going to be infused with poison that would make your hair fall out and would make you vomit everything you ate—or, they would bombard you with more radiation that an atomic bomb blast at Bikini Atoll, and your hair would fall out and the food, blah blah blah, and your life will really suck—unless you go into remission (which wasn't the same thing as being cured), after which you'll freak out every time you felt a pain someplace new, and your dreaded follow-up exams, and the only good thing about your life was that it was going to be a helluva lot shorter. Basically, your physician and your family became lupus deniers to go with cancer, as there were actual treatments for it. But your faith in science and people in white lab coats took a giant hit, which made

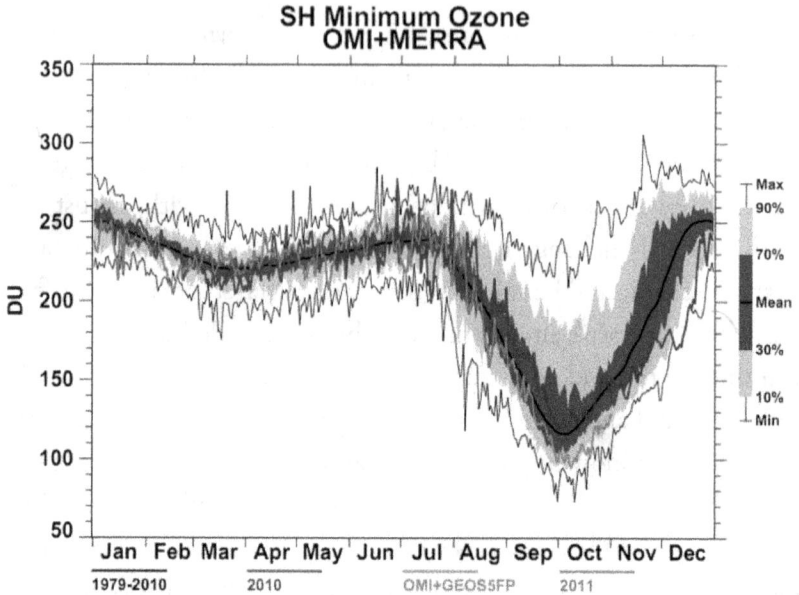

SH Minimum Ozone
OMI+MERRA

you doubt the entire veracity of Milgram's Experiment and how Nazi atrocities have been tied to that Yale research where people turned the voltage up to eleven when white lab-coated fiends directed them to, thus having them believe they were electrocuting strangers.

Yeah, fuck that.

Pink Floyd cloyingly referred to religion as "softly spoken magic spells," which begs the question if any of them had ever read Revelations, which seemed likely. How else did they come up with a song called, "Careful with that Ax, Eugene?" But in any scenario of mass destruction and doom and gloom and the renting of garments, people have always suspected that someone was getting rich if the rest of us were being told what to do, and it was something that we didn't like and who had no use for the solution. Human beings are dysfunctional at their core, so you can't go around preaching horrors that we caused and then deliver the bad news about what we have to give up in order to fix the thing we screwed up in the first place. Self-sacrifice isn't in our DNA, unless people who don't look, sound, or pray like us knock down our buildings—but ask us to use renewable energy or get jabbed in the arm and our collective dander rises faster than the Pillsbury Doughboy's biscuit on Viagra.

So what the scientists *should* have done back in the ozone-layer-panic days was to add all the things we needed to do to combat climate change but substitute the term "ozone layer" for "climate change" or "global warming." We understood that. "Hole, bad. Must fix. Fixing hole, pain in ass, but don't want to end up in fiery death like ants under magnifying glass." Even if the solutions were complicated, if it was to fix one, easily understood thing, we would have done it. We don't want the full body scan showing us everything that is wrong with us. We just want the MRI on our head, revealing the grapefruit-sized tumor. While chemo is about as crappy a treatment as it gets, most of us will do it just to stick around a little while longer to be a burden to someone else. That's the circle of life. So the scientists and climatologists and meteorologists and let's throw in the proctologists for good measure all blew it when, soon after the ozone layer fiasco, they immediately began harping on climate change. Oh sure, some were sounding the alarm back then and they even tied the hole in the ozone layer to it. But we have collective ADD, and just can't focus on more than one disaster at a time. So once the ozone layer reared its ugly, atmosphere-dissolving head, they just should have gathered all of the world's ills into that bucket, sounded one, specific alarm that even the Okie from Muskogee could understand, and stood back to watch our collective altruism kick in. Sure, ozone layer deniers would have cropped up, but that's a much tougher conspiracy to sell as it's so specific and leaves a lot less room for creative, tin-foil hattery. Use the same group-think solution on them. Instead of JFK, 9/11, and climate change, we should all try to get them to fixate only on the Earth being Flat. This hurts no one. They aren't suggesting the Earth needs fixing and shouldbe converted into a globe, and we aren't affected by having them believe that Big Science is lying to us, so let's keep that fire stoked. We should only publicly discuss the Flatness of the Earth and talk about the rest of the really important shit amongst ourselves. That means having the discipline to never, ever bring up any other issues on social media *except* the Earth's shape, and that's all we should allow ourselves to fight over. It's our anesthesia. We put the patient out, and when they wake up, they are none the wiser that we fixed everything. They might feel some discomfort, but everything is going to be OK. So mum's the word. Climate change, anti-vaxx, and any other dimbulb denier group is on double secret probation while we all fix everything. It's a second chance. Let's not blow it!

THE NFL

There's a reason football has become America's Game. It's because there are so few games. In football, your team comes out of the gate and drops the first game and they call the next game a *must win*. Baseball has 162 games, and basketball and hockey about half of that. Almost everybody makes the playoffs, and then you find out how little the regular season mattered because a couple of teams got hot at the end and blew right through the playoffs, and one of those teams ended up winning the championship. So people started tuning out the regular season because it just didn't matter. That doesn't happen with football. At one point, football was fourteen games and only played on Sunday. And then they got greedy. The network created Monday Night Football, believing Mondays were so shitty, people wouldn't mind staying up late and going into work late and hungover—but it wouldn't matter, as they surmised their boss probably also stayed up late and had himself a few (remember, it started during the time when female bosses were a unicorn), and they were right. It was a huge hit, and it just opened the door for more.

The "more" came at a furious pace. The season expanded to sixteen games, they created Monday Night Football on Thursday Night, and then added Sunday Night Football, and now Monday Night Football has two goddamned games and the season is up to seventeen games and—where does it end? It feels like a baseball season, where you turn on your TV on any day and there's an NFL game on. There are some games on Saturday, which were once considered sacrosanct for college football, and they haven't even given it a branding name—it's just a game that happens to be played on Saturday, and isn't that nice? So now, trying to follow your favorite team's schedule is like figuring out how to score in bowling or set up your printer. It's all over the place, and doesn't make any sense, and we don't even know what constitutes a good season anymore. Is anybody going to cheer if their team goes 9–8? I guess maybe if they were 4–12 the year before, but that had a nice, even addition to it. The NFL is a perfect indication of how American corporate minds think: if it's great, more must be better, even if it means watering down the product so it actually gives us less when all is said and done. But our advertisers and rabid fans are happy, so screw it. It's no different than the packaging world for consumer products, when they create a much bigger size but it actually feels as if there is less inside. Anyone who eats potato chips or breakfast cereal understands that. It becomes too confusing to sort it all out, because if you stick with the analogy, if they are blowing it more, they are actually blowing it less, because we are getting less of what we thought we were getting when we were getting less of the more. It's all the "was" of "what will be." Television production of sports entertainment was supposed to be the purest form of pablum for the masses. The idiot box transmits images without a plot, no matter how hard the announcers try to concoct one, and we just watch, drooling on our numbered jerseys while shoveling food into our gobs, which are blaring at us between plays, and the only thing different between this show and *I Love Lucy* reruns is that it's live, original content. If they can ruin sports, and they did, what isn't within their purview to totally fuck up? The Greedheads did exactly what the commentators often tell us during the games: they blew the lead.

NIKE

Everybody recognizes the Nike brand. Sure, now, but that wasn't the case in the 80s. In 1987, they actually laid off one-fifth of their entire workforce. They were marketing their athletic shoes only to those who were already involved in competitive sports, which at that time, represented only about one million potential consumers. Adidas was killing them with their famous athlete endorsements and Run DMC, whose "My Adidas" was released in 1986, causing the rap and hip-hop consumer to rush out and buy them. Nike became desperate. So, they turned to renegade advertising agency, Wieden+Kennedy and their executives, Scott Bedbury and Jerome Conlon, came up with "Just Do It." It was a call to action that didn't necessarily drive consumers to the product, but to their own goals. Everyone had a mountain to climb or a race to run in their own life. Even suburban moms and dads developed their own fitness goals unique to them, and they were finally encouraged to pursue them at their own pace, within the competitive universe that made them feel self-actualized—or at least OK, if you were *doing it*. The professional athlete and kid who grew up as the runt of the litter alike saw the ribbon at the end of the track, and they wanted to hurtle their bodies toward it, break that ribbon, and raise their arms in a V: the heroes of their own lives.

"Just Do It" appealed to those base emotions, and it created a feeling that we could do anything.

And that became the problem.

With new technology in a variety of industries and the DIY ethic inspired by "Just Do It," millions of people began doing the things they always dreamed, such as writing, producing, and editing their own films. Ask any film festival director (like me), and they'll tell you the ability to bypass the very complicated and expensive film format meant that film festival submissions exploded, and festival juries had to now wade through a plethora of crap created by people who were convinced that their unique vision demanded to be seen, adding little bon mots such as "Hollywood would never make this." Well that's Goddamn right! So while submission fee revenues also skyrocketed, so did the hate mail and voicemails left by disappointed filmmakers whose gibberish was rightly rejected. And as technology continued to march ahead, the little non-talented buggers found platforms to actually show their work, such as YouTube and an entire morass of social media sites dedicated to making sure that anyone can be a star in their

own mind for five minutes—down from the once "fifteen minutes." Now, with poorer content comes lesser fame, even with inflation. Those dimbulbs had no idea what working with actual film was like. It often took an entire day or more just to sync up the film and sound, and an edit was cutting the film, so you had to be pretty sure it was what you wanted as it took more cutting to undo it, and not just a few computer keystrokes. You had to mortgage all you had just for the lab costs, and they would hold your film hostage if you were short. And don't even think about what a locked edit in film and making an answer print *cost* in order to show it a film festival, in case you were actually accepted, and then holding your breath as some stranger threaded your film through their projector and you prayed it wouldn't be scratched—which, of course, it was.

The same thing happened in the music and publishing businesses. Anyone could professionally record their nephew's garage band or their daughter's off-key warbling and even use things like Auto-Tune to actually make them sound OK. Expensive recording studios, professional producers, and engineers were no longer a necessity, and now, once again thanks to social media, they all found a place where you—yes, *you*—could hear this totally unknown superstar-in-waiting. Now, not all of them were talentless hacks, and then thanks to shows like *American Idol* and *America's Got Talent,* amateurs could actually audition, get selected, and perform on a show whose ratings meant that millions of people could hear their performances, thus totally circumventing the entire process of begging for live bookings and performing in dive bars, crusty lounges, and Holiday Inn Green Rooms in front of five drunken boors just to hone their talent and actually learn how to perform. And then maybe, just maybe, they could get a minor record deal with local distribution and get the record played at the local college radio station to play a regional college circuit, and prove their chops enough to get a bigger label interested—and even then, the idea of breaking through to a mass audience and producing a hit was *remote*, as it should be.

Most will never have anything close to a hit, but they can show how many likes or clicks they received and, these days, that's almost as good as the filthy lucre itself. Record label artist & repertoire (A&R)

personnel used to frequent all of the live music venues, seeking that one, possible artist that they could sign, thus launching both of their careers. And in the entertainment biz, once you score a hit, no matter how many years or decades between your success, someone will always bank on your replicating it and give you one more chance.

And the same is true of publishing. While there have always been vanity publishers, now anyone can pay to have their book actually professionally packaged, printed, and put up on Amazon for sale (I know, this is ironic). But this actually provides some humor, as far too many people have no idea that the traditional publishing companies don't charge the writer for the privilege of publishing their novel, but actually pay to do so. But these self-indulgent hacks will still proclaim to anyone listening that they have, indeed, received a publishing deal for all their friends to celebrate and be envious of, as they are pressured to first buy and then review their work, memorializing their life's suffering—or worse, their attempt at the penultimate, *Great American Novel*.

At least professional sports teams who, originally, were the target audience for companies like Nike, had the good sense to retain the usual method of getting their athletes via the draft. No kid's fever dream of catching a wicked line drive in the stands, causing an excited and amazed scout in the stands to scream, "Sign that kid up!" ever happened. But "Just Do It" found its permanent way into both the lexicon and zeitgeist, and it continues to inspire the untalented into putting their shit out there and clogging up all the distribution channels of just about everything we see and hear on our laptops—and the end is nowhere in sight.

Artists used to have to be developed and nurtured. John Cassavetes, one of the greatest independent filmmakers ever, had to drag his reels in their heavy metal cans from theater to theater in the hopes of finding one that might screen his work and then pray that it might be reviewed, which could lead to more screenings and possibly a distribution deal and the paying back of the lab bills. And eating. Musical artists, even if they were scouted by an A&R guy, were given the slow route to fame and fortune. Their deals actually had them paying the record company back for recording and tour costs. And the labels would never push radio to actually play their songs, because they knew that they only got one chance to get it right (after payola was considered a crime). So it would often be several albums into their career before the label heard the development enough to declare a song worthy of a hit, and only then would they put the apparatus behind the artist in the hopes of manufacturing a hit single, which would then require a bigger tour and finally the machine kicked in. Publishing had a long track record of the most famous writers we know having to wade through a litany of rejection letters and a crapload of bad jobs before a publishing house would take a chance, and they then become the Kurt Vonnegut or Stephen King we all adore.

So congratulations, Nike. Your company is worth a gazillion dollars, but you still blew it. Now excuse me while I research for the best self-publishing options for whiney screeds, manifestos, and communiques.

BURGER KING

Dovetailing with Nike's "Just Do It" came Burger King's 1976 slogan, "Have It Your Way." Ostensibly, this was the counterpoint to the rigidity of McDonald's, who not only refused to do anything to upset the uniformity of their manufacturing system, they even made us learn exactly what was on their Big Mac, which, as we all know, consisted of "two all-beef patties, special sauce, lettuce, pickles, cheese, onions and a sesame seed bun." And just as "Just Do it" did, "Have It Your Way" was yet another aspect of the advertising age to give us all false hope. First of all, we really can't "have it our way." Never could, never will. We all got used to the *no substitutions* on every Chinese menu. There is something actually freeing about not actually having to think or make anything closely resembling a decision when it comes to ordering fast food, or anything for that matter. Now we know why the caged bird sings.

Amazon Prime customers rarely get their packages with next-day delivery. It's almost a dare: "whatcha gonna do about it?" Well, what are we going to do about it? Go to an Amazon Distribution Center in our area and Karen it up by demanding to see the manager? All we'll see are a ton of underpaid, overworked drones, doing their damned best to sort out the massive amount of parcels they handle now that Covid has made the entire country La-Z-Boy computer shoppers.

Dominos once promised us our pizzas in thirty minutes or it's free, and how did that turn out? We don't want it to be quick. We don't want it our way. And we sure as hell ain't gonna "just do it." We have long ago lost the ability to make any meaningful choices in our lives. Not in food, relationships, work, or anything. Our brains have been overtaxed ever since the information age took over, and we need *fewer* choices, not more. It's part of the reason our political landscape is such a horror show. We wouldn't know what to do with an honest, uncorrupted politician if we ever got one, so we might as well continue with our eenie-meenie-miney-moe approach for the lesser of two evils. We make chicken salad out of chicken shit, and often, we can't even do that, so we just hold our noses and shovel down the chicken shit and convince ourselves how yummy it was because that "spoonful of sugar" method sure as hell didn't work. We don't even know how to watch TV anymore. There are now oodles of streaming services, and who actually understands how to maneuver through those? Top shows were reportedly cancelled before we were ever aware of their existence. Even young people are listening with rapt attention as the Baby Boomers wax poetically about the day of three networks, impossible-to-tune-in UHF and VHF stations, and PBS, which nobody watched but everybody donated to just to get the nifty tote bag.

We have long been fooled by the concept of choice and having it our way. We can't. We never could. And it's getting too hard even to think about wanting to.

It's why I don't believe that the "Pro-Life" crowd is that at all. If they were actually pro-life, they would advocate for a national health insurance plan that also covers daycare, education, and all sorts of programs that help ensure the life and potential happiness of a child. So what they really are is anti-choice. The thought of women having the right and actual ability to exercise such a choice is frightening to them. But by that measure, I don't really believe that white supremacists or white nationalists are all about skin color. They just prefer a monochromatic world for its simplicity, not its history. Same with religion—religion is a choice, so better eliminate that as well. It explains why America is hurtling towards fascism and authoritarian rule. Loki said it best in

the first *Avengers* film, when he stood toward a crowd, unironically in Germany where he was pulling a caper, and said, "You were made to be ruled."

So basically, "Have It Your Way" really means "do it my way." Humans in general, but Americans in particular, seem to have an innate need to have shortcuts to critical thinking, and the best way to do that is to eliminate choice as often as possible, to reduce the actual amount of time one needs to think. Even the Sylvester Stallone film, *Demolition Man,* figured that out when they presented a future where the only restaurant was Taco Bell. Personally, I would prefer the only choice be White Castle, but that sounds suspiciously like I made a decision, so I shall defer to those more qualified to make them— and that is probably some supercomputer with a learning algorithm located somewhere beneath a mountain in Wyoming.

MTV'S THE REAL WORLD

We could actually go back to when MTV itself began, but while the remnants of quick edits remain, the essence of a music channel doesn't. But their foray into non-musical programming, or what they believed they were **MUSIC TELEVISION®** presenting as "documentary television," continues its impact today and, unfortunately, will probably never end. The actual idea of shooting people documentary-style occurred much earlier, in the 70s, with PBS's *An American Family*, which brought the Loud Family into our living rooms. And if you want to be picky, *Candid Camera* did it earlier than that with the eponymous show. But the difference there, and with all of the reality TV shows that followed, was that the people on Candid Camera had no idea that they were on camera, so their reactions were the real real. Ask any documentary filmmaker how the camera changes the gestalt of what is really taking place. Even the first famous documentary, *Nanook of the North*, had its participants do things they wouldn't ordinarily do to make for more exciting footage. And ask Bob Dylan if his utter destruction of his implied rival, Donovan, in *Don't Look Back* wasn't him working the cameras for his own benefit instead of a natural interaction among old and potentially new friends.

So now the network that gave us Duran Duran, The Buggles, and The Vapors is shoving their version of reality down our throats, because, as they did in their first season in 1992 where they set the cast up in a hip, SoHo loft:

"This is the true story of seven strangers, picked to live in a house, work together, and have their lives taped. Find out what happens when people stop being polite, and start getting real...The Real World!"

The only thing true about it would be the total flooding of the airwaves of more and more insipid reality, from *Survivor* and *Big Brother* to the virus of all viruses, *The Apprentice*, and we all know what that gave us.

But wait, there's more.

We are now infested with influencers, and to make that thought even more vile, they are actually broken down into subcategories:[*]

Mega-Influencers

Mega influencers are the people with a vast number of followers on their social networks. Although there are no fixed rules on the boundaries between the different types of followers, a common view is that mega-influencers have more than one million followers on at least one social platform.

Macro-Influencers

Macro-influencers are one step down from the mega-influencers, and maybe more accessible as influencer marketers. You would consider people with followers in the range between 40,000 and one million followers on a social network to be macro-influencers.

This group tends to consist of two types of people. They are either B-grade celebrities who haven't yet made it to the big time, or they are successful online experts, who have built up more significant followings than the typical micro-influencers.

---

[*]   Source—https://www.pukket.com/

Micro-Influencers

Micro-influencers are ordinary, everyday people who have become known for their knowledge about some specialist niche. As such, they have usually gained a sizable social media following amongst devotees of that niche. Of course, it is not just the number of followers that indicates a level of influence; it is the relationship and interaction that a micro-influencer has with his or her followers.

Although views differ, you could consider micro-influencers as having between 1,000 and 40,000 followers on a single social platform.

Nano-Influencers

The newest influencer-type to gain recognition is the nano-influencer. These people only have a small number of followers, but they tend to be experts in an obscure or highly specialized field. You can think of nano-influencers as being the proverbial big fish in a small pond. In many cases, they have fewer than 1,000 followers, but these will be keen and interested followers, willing to engage with the nano-influencer and listen to his/her opinions.

Had enough? I hope not, as we now have to sort out the above gibberish into types, which are:

- Bloggers
- YouTubers
- Podcasters
- Social Posts Only

I thought it wise not to go into the nonsensical descriptions for the categories, because it goes on and on into things such as level of influence, key opinion leaders, and, God-help-us-all, Chromo-Influencers, which can be both a subset and a category.

Are you following this?

The day MTV premiered on August 1, 1981 could be the beginning of the throughline for all this mishigas, but when they only played music videos, it was actually tolerable. Some bands/videos were great, others, not so much, but they didn't infiltrate every aspect of our lives—especially once the online universe decided to do that for us. But the current ability for any schmuck to actually have a podium from which to extoll their opinions, expertise, and just pure twaddle has gone way past the "annoying" mark and into "mass stupidity."

It's too easy to blame social media and the tech giants that created all of the social media platforms, or Sir Timothy John Berners-Lee, or even Al Gore for all the horrors that have oozed from Facebook, Twitter, etc. While there is plenty of blame for the Zuckerbergs or that yutz, Tom Anderson whose smiling visage became our first friend on the practically extinct MySpace, the real villain was the company and production team that unleashed *The Real World* with nothing but a profit motive. At least Mark and Tom started out slightly altruistic but became as corrupt as any of us would have if given the keys to the kingdom and an insane amount of fuck-you money. And that fell squarely in the laps of the people behind *The Real World*. Now, if during a very special episode they hid a pit viper in one of their toney locations just to see the ensuing fun, or a hidden quicksand trap shows up one day at the front stoop, now that's entertainment, and a can-you-top-this race to the emergency room would have been glorious to watch. Make one of the seasonal locations Attica and then, yeah, we'll watch when people stop being polite and start getting real right up the wazoo. Hope the network stocked you up with plenty of cartons of cigarettes, bitch!

THE DECADE THE MUSIC DIED

If the music of the 80s was projected on an oscilloscope, it would produce a typical sine wave, going up into peaks and down into valleys. It gave us a ton of synth pop and Brit pop, such as Depeche Mode, New Order, OMD, Soft Cell, Human League, Kajagoogoo, Gary Numan and Yello, whose song, "Oh Yeah" seemed to have been placed on every soundtrack, which sounds suspiciously like something Russia would do (Hmmm...they *were* Swiss). Now there was also arena rock, pumped out by Aerosmith, who somehow made it out of the 70s, Van Halen, and Def Leppard. We had wonderful, overwrought pop, where every song was some kind of desperate plea from bands like Tears for Fears and Thompson Twins. And rounding out the decade were the inimitable hair bands, such as Ratt, Poison, RattPoison, PoisonRatts, Men Without Ratts, and Mötley Crüe. Those bands came out all tattooed and not only sang about having sex with your teenaged daughters, but actually did so.

Mom, too.

They really did.

The Ratt bastards.

None of this was a bad thing, but something weird happened towards the end of the decade and that's when radio and the charts became dominated by an endless loop of disposable dance music, with such vomit-inducing artists as C+C Music Factory, Technotronic,

Young MC, and the biggest fugazi of all time, Milli Vanilli. And though it wasn't released until 1993, it represented the horror genre when Haddaway's "What is Love" came out. It hit number one in almost every country, inspired an ongoing skit on Saturday Night Live with Will Ferrell and Chris Kataan wearing day-glo suits and nodding their heads to the rhythm so hard they decided to spin it off into its own, wretched movie.

But as Newton taught us, with every action there is an equal and opposite reaction. And the pushback came from the daily overcast, over-caffeinated Pacific Northwest/Seattle music scene. With a daily threat of rain, it was no wonder that coffee bars were birthed from this region and, with the upper pumping in everybody's veins, a scene developed, consisting of throwback muscular guitar players and titanium-throated singers. In all fairness, it wasn't so much a scene but a bunch of bands that switched partners more than the cool kids in high school. They had Sub Pop Records, a label that hosted virtually every artist from the area, and the originals—the ones that actually influenced and inspired the ones that made it were The Melvins, Tad, Green River, Bundle of Hiss, Hammerbox, 7 Year Bitch, and The Young Fresh Fellows. Mother Love Bone was the first poised to break out until their lead singer, Andrew Wood, saw the needle and the damage done and OD'd. But from the ashes of that band sprang the one-off Temple of the Dog, which then divided into Pearl Jam and Soundgarden. They were soon joined by Alice in Chains, Screaming Trees, Mudhoney, and The Posies. But of course, it was Nirvana that blew the entire lid off the supposed scene and suddenly, they had the nom de plume of Grunge. The overall sound of artists and bands that were miles apart from the dance acts was then labeled "alternative," and radio started playing all kinds of music that before was relegated, to what the Minneapolis band, The Replacements (or Place Mats, as they were often called), named *the left of the dial.* The music trades, Billboard and R&R (Radio & Records), created their own chart, Modern Rock, but those bands crossed over into the top 40—the chart counted down by the likes of Casey Kasem and Shadoe Stevens.

Suddenly, The Cure and bands who were descendants of radio staples such as Camper Van Beethoven and Hüsker Dü found themselves getting actual radio airplay, and even charting. It was a fresh new world, and MTV had their own hot version of the music with 120 Minutes. New Jersey radio station WDRE changed formats into modern rock, followed by other stations that were once AOR (Album-Oriented Rock), playing mostly classic hits from The Beatles, Led Zeppelin and the like, which now might actually spin a tune from The Happy Mondays, The Poppinjays or Catherine Wheel.

But once again, Newton had to rear his ugly head and the opposite reaction inevitably occurred. Once the alternative became mainstream, the corporations did their thing. The labels signed basically every band they thought were grunge or alternative regardless of talent. And the massive radio station corporations, like Clear Channel (now iHeartRadio) and Susquehanna, centralized their programming with silly names such as The River, or The Wolf, or whatever clever name they thought sounded both edgy *and* non-threatening. So the promo people from record labels—the men and women who went from station to station in their territory, trying to get the program directors to add their latest single to their playlist and then get it moved up into light, medium, and heavy rotation in order to first get and then keep their bullet on the charts, were phased out. Compilations from sales and airplay were no longer needed. Music was basically franchised, like fast food. No matter what market you drove through, the music would be the same. This basically blew up the entire system so that an artist's number one revenue stream was—now get this—*ringtones*.

Yes, when you pay 99 cents to download music to play on the worst speaker out there just for those few seconds so anyone within earshot can discover just how cool you are, you know you are in The End Times. That's how artists are making bank. Now don't you feel like the most going-against-the-grain, individual, not-a-lemming dude or dudette out there? So the lesson (or irony) to be learned was that once there is an actual movement toward something new and fresh and free of constraints, the people who have been given the responsibility of what the country listens to from car radios will fucking kill it and mine all the money they can from it, while destroying all the joy we had for that briefest of moments. But it didn't really matter. The record store is dead, so no more shopping inside a place and fingering your way through the bins while the PA plays whatever the owner wants you to end up buying because he or she knows it's great and you don't—not yet anyway—until the snarky salespeople point and laugh at your lame choices you sheepishly hand over at the register. They will get you to buy enough good shit that, under your breath—mixed in with the curses—will be a huge "thank you" following your Moment of Ridicule. Radio is also dead, and we listen to programming brought to us by Pandora or Spotify or Sirius XM, where we can choose music like we do news, going with Fox or MSNBC to see what we know we already like—so no being exposed to something new and different because that will upset our equilibrium and kick our OCD into high gear, and the drugs for that just don't mix with all the other drugs we are taking for the smorgasbord of ills we suffer and can't calm down as we used to by listening to the radio and waiting to hear something new that can actually excite us, just for a moment.

And sure, we made fun of so many of those artists and bands from the 80s, but we never accused them of rehashing old ground. Dexy's Midnight Runners, Pete Shilling, Nina, Pet Shop Boys, Spandau Ballet, A-Ha, Kraftwerk, and *Alles Klar Herr Kommisar* by both Falco *and* After the Fire didn't sound like each other, and some were only around for a cup of coffee (hopefully not from Starbucks).

The alternative genre even spawned two outdoor concert festivals: Lollapalooza and Lilith Fair. Lollapalooza was the brainchild of Perry Farrell, lead singer of Jane's Addiction, and it's first incarnation was in 1991. It brought together artists and bands from grunge, hard rock, heavy metal, alternative, rap, hip hop, industrial and electronica. It also featured visual arts and nonprofit organizations. Spin Magazine called it the greatest tour in the last 35 years and Farrell coined the term *Alternative Nation* to describe the tour and its impact. But as the first tour included mostly artists that had not yet made their name in the industry, the follow-up included mostly bands that had already achieved success. So the evolution of corrupting the difference into the normal happened that quickly. The ticket and food prices skyrocketed. Lollapalooza died in 1997. But it was revived in 2003—and then COVID-19 killed it again in 2020. Even if it continues, it will just be another money-grubbing, soul-crushing event, and we've had far too many of those.

Lilith Fair began in 1997 and was created by Sarah McLachlan before she became ubiquitously known for making you cry by watching her commercials for saving abused animals. The concept was simple enough: female performers get the short end of the stick when it comes to concert appearance and promotion, so they made their own concert series and promoted it

Morrisey once sang, "We Hate It When Our Friends Become Successful," and that's what happened to the music business. In the 80s and early 90s, so many artists and bands of all different stripes had success as we suddenly became open to the concept of something new and different, even if it was often cheesy. So the money comes in and waters it down so badly that it all sucks and no one is successful anymore unless your phone is playing their song.

JUNK BONDS

There is so much blame to throw around the banking and capital center as a whole, and the unbelievable number of times we have had to collectively bend over and take it up the wazoo by the cretins that manage, invest, and basically decide for all of us where our money goes is ridiculous. The powerful financial-investment banking firms designated to their franchises (that were basically mall kiosks) told us how and where to funnel our money in multiple schemes that had them always coming out on top and us, much less so. But we're using the overarching term "junk bonds" because it contains the word "junk": an apt description for the veritable shit-storm Wall Street and the nefarious greedheads behind the schemes that screw us all create while they party on their yachts.

The actual technical name for "junk bonds" is "high yield bonds," and it stems from the fact that issuers with poor credit ratings have very few options with which to screw us over, so they offer us bonds with far higher yields than issuers with better credit ratings do. So of course there is greater risk for investors, and those investors—let's call them "suckers"—end up with junk instead of bonds with any real value. Your bookie or OBT window person would simply call them "long shots," and yes, if they come in, you get a lot more money, but there is a reason that your horse named Glue Factory went off at 750–1 at Aqueduct.

Junk bonds were issued by companies known as Fallen Angels

(another great name for a horse you should never bet on) as their credit rating dropped faster than the mic at a dozens contest. And the twatwaffle we mostly associate junk bonds with was Michael Milken. He worked at the investment bank, Drexel Burnham Lambert, which had so many names—it merged more times than Holland Tunnel traffic. They thought he was adorable, so they patted him on his dead-weasel toupee, gave him a small amount of capital to create his high-yield division, and never gave him a second thought. That was, until they noticed he was earning 100percent almost overnight on the capital they fronted him. So they waved their red cape—olé!—and gave him carte blanche, and he moved his operation to Beverly Hills. His mantra was simple: why fuck over a limited amount of people and institutions when you can go all full chicanery and bilk a shit ton by investing in a crapload of companies on the brink of insolvency? This was, and continues to be, the mark of capitalism unleashed. If your low-rated company suddenly gets a massive infusion of cash, boy-oh-boy, it will suddenly look fabulous and the price of those seemingly junky bonds will reach heavenly heights. He bridged the gap from President Jimmy Carter's stagflation to President Ronald Reagan's supply-side economics—which his one-time opponent and eventual VP rightfully called "voodoo economics."

Because the junk bonds were, well, so junky, their cheapness attracted all sorts of marks to the carnival and demand quickly outstripped supply. This made them even more volatile and risky, something Milken actually became gleeful over as he thought (I mean he really did) that the precarious ledge he and his investors were sitting on actually brought them stability. He used his windfall to be the granddaddy of corporate raiders, using the cash to buy out other companies on the brink and anchored with enormous debt. Reagan's America was giddy, with its laissez-faire attitude toward money and turned a blind eye that Milken and other junk bond issuers were basically defrauding their clients and had built a giant pyramid scheme. It was a bubble, a word that would and continues to creep into our everyday lexicon when we discuss money and how we're losing it by the bushel.

The first domino fell when Ivan Boesky, a big-time hustler with ties to Milken, was investigated by then New York DA Rudy Giuliani, before he became the total assclown we know today. When the rats started to desert the sinking ship, Drexel Lambert Burnham went all Nike and put out an ad that said "Junk Bonds Keep America Fit." In September 1988, the SEC sued Drexel and Milken for a multitude of violations including insider trading, manipulation of stock prices, and inaccurate record-keeping. Most serious of all were allegations of fraud and racketeering. The jig was up, and in 1990, turned out by his employer who had to pay 650 million to help with the securities investigation, Milken was found guilty, levied a fine of 250 million and spent some time in the hoosegow. Unfortunately, while this made headlines in all of the financial and Wall Street news and other money-focused media organizations, a few other small incidents at that time, such as the Fall of the Berlin Wall, the release of Nelson Mandela, and Margaret Thatcher got the heave-ho off the front page for an ill-advised poll tax.

So sure, some millionaires were temporarily inconvenienced but they usually bounced back with another money scheme, which was their version of Tommy John Surgery. One revenue stream blows up, just replace it with another—usually from the body of some middle-class schmuck—and retake the mound, throwing spitballs to see how long you can get away with it...again. The 80s saw Congress deregulate the Savings and Loan industry, which created more ways to save money on junk products, some of which remain today—such as the adjustable-rate mortgage. It worked on the same principle as junk bonds as weaker savings and loan institutions attracted deposits by offering high yield rates, which they could only afford by investing themselves in risky investments and loans. That enabled them to grow at a whopping 56 percent rate as opposed to the 24 percent rates commercial banks rose during the same period from 1982–1985. The savings and loan debacle had major Wall Street firms buying up their loans at 60–90 percent of their value and then bundling them effectively with government-backed bonds by virtue of Ginny Mae, Freddie Mac, or Fannie Mae guarantees, and that clusterfuck would rear its ugly head in the form of a slew of bankruptcies and foreclosures, resulting in a gaggle of people getting evicted as their mortgages kept getting bundled and sold and resold until they had no idea who held the note or when the note was coming due.

And still, we learned nothing. Clinton repealed Glass-Steagall in 1999, which let banks get even larger until they were considered "too big to fail," and that led to the subprime mortgage meltdown, forcing us to bail their asses out. And we then hippity-hopped to the DotCom bubble where, once again, companies had their actual value overestimated because they really didn't produce anything except get a shitload of us using them, when those ambiguous, shadowy figures known as "financial analysts" decided that they're worth billions even though they couldn't actually show that type of revenue. Likes and clicks didn't mean bucks, so everything started to fall apart and, as usual, the lower and middle classes bore the financial burden while the banks and analysts just skipped their merry way into the next scheme, such as hedge funds.

If there was any nome de plume we should attach to the decades of misery foisted upon us by a group of the shadiest operators who hide behind the brick and mortar of respectable-looking buildings, it should be Blewgate. Of course, deciding who really is to blame—*All the President's Men* or the rest of us Ralph Kramdens desperately seeking our next get-rich-quick caper—is the tricky part.

Ostensibly not as big a deal, but the perfect metaphor for greed and blame, the Crazy Eddie electronics meltdown was another canary in a coal mine that drew a typical throughline about how things work today. Eddie Antar's eponymous, Tristate electronics store chain was often imitated, never duplicated, due to the antics of New York DJ Dr. Jerry Carroll who ended each commercial aping the old radio car salesman pitches by doing a coked-up "His prices are insane!" after each spot. Crazy Eddie started the entire "Christmas in August" sale schtick. Those fuel-injected, lowbrow, lowlife ads totaled more than 7500 in the 80s and he sold so much gear, including Atari Game Systems, that when Warner Communications, who owned Atari, sued Eddie for copyright infringement for his use of a Superman-type version of Crazy Eddie (they also were the distributors of Superman Comics), the suit was quietly settled.

Even though he was regional, Crazy Eddie was imitated by Dan Ackroyd on an early *Saturday Night Live* fake commercial, featuring Crazy Ernie. HBO's *Not Necessarily the News* had Crazy Ollie, taking on Col. Oliver North as the frenetic pitchman for used weapons at bargain basement prices. And Daryl Hannah's mermaid from the 1984 film *Splash* freaked out when she first viewed a Crazy Eddie ad.

But Crazy Eddie might have had some Mafia training, as he kept two sets of books and paid his employees under the table to hide how much cash was actually pouring in and laundering it in Israeli banks. He did what any financial analyst might have cooked up: take the company public, and his 1984 IPO sold at $8 per share but soon ballooned to $75. Eddy recruited his cousin, Sam, who was a prominent accountant, to further launder the money, and Sam came up with what became known as The Panama Pump. The money he sent to Israeli banks was transferred to Panamanian banks with false account names, which then were paid out to Crazy Eddie. They also engaged in inventory fraud to inflate the stores' value, and that level of fraud increased value from $3 million to $10 up to as high as $12 million. If nothing else, Eddie Antar couldn't be accused of false advertising; he really was crazy.

But Eddie forgot the gangster creed: keep you friends close and your enemies closer. Of course, he did it his own, Crazy Eddie way by actually making his friends his enemies—basically, his wife.

He had an affair, and his wife and sister caught him in the act. One lesson of operating a successful scam is to be able to depend on family members who knew where the bodies were buried. Infidelity was not the best idea to ensure mouths would stay shut.

The fraud became harder to disguise as more and more people began to talk about it. Eddie then faked his own resignation as company CEO as the stock continued to tumble. When a Houston-based businessman initiated a hostile takeover of the company, more and

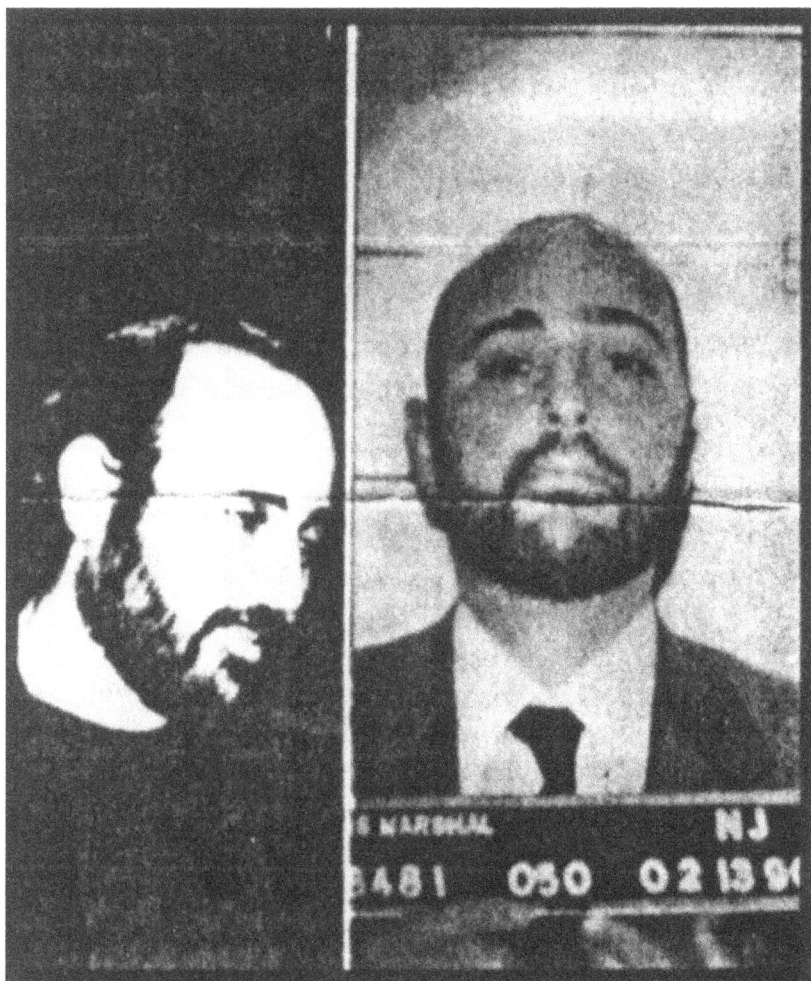

more of Crazy Eddie's fraud came to light, triggering a slew of lawsuits. Efforts to stymie the takeover failed, and the Houston businessman's buyout was complete, uncovering an even greater level of fraud then at first thought. The inventory was short by a trifling $80 million. Vendors began pounding on the doors demanding liquidation of whatever stock there was so they could at least get back pennies on the dollar, but Eddie fooled them all by pretending not to be home, the scamp. By the end of 1989, Crazy Eddie was completely shuddered and liquidated, and the late-night airwaves and the shut-ins who watched it were much the poorer, but not quite as poor as Eddie himself.

Former employees and family started spilling to the Feds and soon, Eddie Antar had the SEC after him for securities fraud and insider trading and jaywalking and rapid and incoherent speech and tearing the label off the bottom of the mattress. When he failed to appear in court, an arrest warrant was issued and he surrendered to US Marshalls but no-showed his next court appearance, so the jig was up. They froze his assets as Eddie fled to Israel on a fake passport, but it only delayed the inevitable. He was extradited, and he and one of his brothers were found guilty—but they won on appeal. The prosecuting attorney labeled Eddie "the Darth Vader of Capitalism." He finally got eight years.

But with all the publicity the trials produced, an investment firm tried to revive the chain and purchased the Crazy Eddie trademark.

In the early 90s, Eddie's grandkids again tried to revive the insanity by creating an online store, but it failed. Others continued to try and resurrect it, but none ever worked. By 2018, the Crazy Eddie trademark was abandoned. Bits and pieces of the type of hyper, hyperbolic advertising remain and then disappear as quickly as they pop up, like a Madison Avenue version of Whack-A-Mole. But Crazy Eddie blew it for all of us who were hooked on deals at insane prices, and while the concept of defrauding consumers, investors, and the government continues, none can do it with the panache of Crazy Eddie. He died in 2016 at age 68. Rumor has it that he started the trend of two-for-one burial sites at your local franchise cemetery.

HMOs

Once upon a time, universal health care was something that interested both Democrats and at least some Republicans. In 1943, individuals were actually discouraged from buying private health insurance by making health care premiums deductible to employers and not individuals. The Right was happy, as it was giving tax breaks to business, and the Left was mollified as it at least gave some health care access to workers. In 1965, Congress established Medicare, making private health insurance to seniors almost obsolete. But that led to a feeding frenzy by both patient enrollment and doctor-advocating, and health costs began to skyrocket. Ted Kennedy began advocating for government-paid, universal health care plans, as most of the Western civilized world had done. In 1971, reincarnated skunk-ape Richard Nixon had a conversation with his syphilitic, monkey-dung of an Assistant to the President on Domestic Affairs, John Ehrlichman. They discussed Kaiser Permanente's idea for a Health Maintenance Organization, but Nixon was having difficulty getting the Nattering Nabob Vice President Agnew to grasp the concept until Monkey-dung mentioned that Kaiser's was a profit grab for the private center based on the radical idea of "the less care given, the more dollar signs appear," which got Nixon's hearty approval. And the Left spread their cheeks and took it up the chute and helped pass the HMO Act in 1973. So between Medicare and the HMO Act, the market for affordable health insurance disappeared into other people's bank accounts. The maze encountered in managed-care bureaucracies couldn't be solved by *Flowers for Algernon* mice, chasing down their favorite cheese. Republican Dennis Haster, whose tenure as Speaker of the House was derailed due to his ethics violations for paying hush money to cover up his little child molestation problems (of which he would later be convicted), actually advocated for Medical Savings Accounts (MSAs) that offered every patient a choice to purchase health insurance as an individual—either through an employer or through government—by legalizing MSAs for all Americans (MSAs were previously restricted to a small group of self-employed, uninsured, small-business people, and several hundred thousand Medicare recipients). Hillary Clinton and Ted Kennedy were against MSAs as they felt that it would siphon off the young and healthy patients and thus blow the lid off of costs for the rest of us sickly curmudgeons fast-approaching get-off-my-lawn-hood. So the one time a really good idea regarding health care came from a Republican in the past fifty years, it had to originate from the poster child for your creepy uncle who likes babysitting way too much.

Health care costs increased 399 percent after the HMO Act passed, followed by more employers quitting the benefit of offering health care to their employees. In 1993, Hillary Clinton, appointed by her hubby, chaired a 600-person panel of experts who got busy at their word processors and vomited up a 1340-page, 240,000-word proposal which was a byzantine offering of universal health care that was so ponderous, nobody actually read it to decide if it was any good. It didn't help that Republicans hated the Clintons for constantly stealing their thunder on programs such as Welfare-to-Work and balancing the budget, all the while appealing to middle America for their peccadilloes and love of fast food and fast women (at least by Bill Clinton). In 2010, Obama signed into law the Affordable Care Act which handled such problems as pre-existing conditions and allowing dependent children to stay on their parents' insurance until they got so sick of their music and whining, they finally got the boot. Obama did wuss out in offering a public option—a true universal health care plan. The entire concept actually came from the Far-Right Heritage Foundation, who through individual mandates showed the type of personal responsibility that Conservatives were always yapping about. The idea was tried when Republican Mitt Romney got elected Governor of Massachusetts and instituted the exact same plan. He called it Commonwealth Care, and there was much rejoicing. But the mere fact that Obama was the one who rammed it through during the short window when he had majorities in both Congressional chambers caused Republicans conniptions, and thus they swore by all that was holy to repeal and replace it, though they never gave an inkling of what it would be replaced with, and so it never was—at least not at the moment this manifesto was being banged out in anger.

So who gets the Fickle Finger of Fuck You? Who blew it on this one?

Politicians are low-hanging fruit. Even when they're good, a huge percentage of us believe they suck and, for the most part, we're right—but as we continue to vote the swine in, we could give a unanimous thumbs-down to the whole lot of us—every person who voted, and every person who didn't. That shotgun approach to blame sure is satisfying...in the short term.

Thirty-two out of the total of thirty-three Western Democracies have chosen universal health care, and have had decades to go in another direction, but none have pulled the trigger. And yes, in case you were wondering, that single idiot holding out for some unicorn health care system that makes everyone giddy is *us*. Obviously, no system is perfect. The People of Massachusetts love Commonwealth Care, and nobody cared that ventriloquist dummy Mitt Romney was the one that did it, or that the entire concept came from a Far-Right think tank that touts themselves as the only ones advocating for free enterprise, limited government, individual freedom, traditional American values, and a strong national defense.

We have had decades of watching other countries all fall in line with the idea, and none of them have 86'd it yet, so despite the constant accusations from so many of us who know that one Canadian or Frenchman or brooding, whiny person from Costa Rica who lives to regale us with tales of long lines, and how so many of them snake into the US when the operation involves the heart of liver or some other somewhat vital organ, universal health care—or socialized medicine—has the approval of the masses. In 2015, the Kaiser Family Foundation found that medical bills made 1 million adults declare bankruptcy. Its survey found that 26 percent of Americans aged 18 to 64 struggled to pay medical bills. According to the US Census, that's 52 million adults. The survey found that 2 percent, or 1 million, said they declared bankruptcy that year. In 2011, Debt.org published that people aged 55 and older account for 20 percent of total filings. So we go broke at an alarming level due to health care costs. For citizens of the remaining 32 other countries, not so much.

There was a time when many doctors were happily driving around town in their Cadillacs, and Lincolns, and the occasional Porsche, but they still made house calls with their ubiquitous, little black bags in tow. They often accepted items in trade, such as giant, inedible lobsters or a tip on a pony at Suffolk Downs. Now they're miserable, and nurses are miserable, and we sure as hell are miserable...and sick. Very, very sick.

Not to make another chapter about McDonald's or fast food in general, but they are a distinct culprit. One out of every 3 Americans are obese, and the majority of them eat frequently at fast food restaurants. And as the number of fast food restaurants increases, so did the number of hospitalized, obese Americans, causing a vicious circle. But the franchises' popularity accompanied the increasing pressures felt by Middle Americans to get things done both at work and home, and time was short to cram in both. When we're not eating out at the Colonel, we're yelling at our microwave Salisbury steak dinner to cook faster, because three minutes for a dinner whose ingredients contain a whole lot of stuff but very little actual food is just too darn long. And back to the "Just Do It" mentality, advertisers started targeting their ads to children to harass their parents to take them to Mickey D's, to the point that getting them to shut their gobs with a mouthful of cheesoid and textured vegetable protein became the lesser of two evils—a noisy brat, or a teenager who was allocated their own zip code. And that isn't to fat-shame them. When you're promised all kinds of toys along with the delicious mouthful of grease and whatever else is in there, you're going to get into a lather until your demands are met, and Mom and Dad are too stressed out with their own financial melt-down that they stopped arguing about how to feed their family for ten dollars in just ten minutes a long time ago. So even though fast food consumption is finally declining and the franchises that are still thriving have added numerous healthy choices to their menus, the damage had already been done. We still have a legion of humans with a myriad of health problems, such as diabetes, hypertension, and anything else a circulatory system of sludge will cause. Many hospitals stopped referring to their patients as "patients" and started calling them "repeat customers." Eat poorly, have your heart attack or stroke, demand the problem get fixed, and, as Steely Dan sang, "Do It Again."

We're a nation of pre-existing conditions, looking for a way of paying those bills now bogging us down, and that doesn't include all the mental health issues that just being an American can cause. We are all basically born suffering from PTSD. It's become genetic.

The Evangelicals will point to what they feel is the destruction of the family unit that led to all of these ills, such as two-paycheck families, divorce, and homosexuality and all the alphabet letters that group now owns. They think if we only went back to "Dad works, Mom babysits and cooks, and everyone goes to church, not a synagogue or mosque but a *church*," then all will be well, including our health and the pressing need for any of us to have to sweat over our insurance premiums.

Of course, we tried that, and died, quite frequently, by age fifty-six, and the life insurance barely covered the funeral expenses, and junior grew up to be draft-dodging Beatnik or Hippie or whatever label the older generation labeled him so they could point the finger at *him* for blowing everything.

So which is it? Religion? Profit? Gastronomical? Political? Who or what screwed the gerbil regarding our inability to stay healthy and then pay for it? It was fun in the 60s to just say *Society* and everybody knew what you meant, but that doesn't work so well these days. Advertising could get the nod, too. They figured out how to make the worst-looking food on Earth look like *Babette's Feast,* and we believed that buying a pair of Nikes would whittle our waistlines and arm flab to acceptable levels, and if you were one of the few who didn't fall for it, give yourself a pat on the back—but don't strain your shoulder, as that isn't covered in your policy. So I'm going to pull this out of my ass and hope that doesn't count as a pre-existing condition and say: the Gold Rushes during America's Frontier Days were responsible.

Huh?

The San Francisco and Dahlonega Gold Rushes gave Americans their first actual taste of the possibilities of power and real wealth. Once people discovered that a shiny rock (in Georgia, locals from Dahlonega often joke that their town's name translated from Cherokee means "the shiny rock valuable to the White Man but useless to us") could change your fortunes, money became the country's Holy Grail. Sure, the Gold Rushes occurred well before 1969, but the gauntlet was thrown down then for the cretins like Kaiser, Milken ,and Crazy Eddy to pick up, along with the plethora of financial institutions that have been sticking it to us for decades. People killed themselves and others just to possess gold or any other precious metal, so should anyone be surprised when a commodity that we all want and need—good health—would be used as a profit incentive? We've spent billions on items that squeeze our thighs together, and metal objects that we pick up and put down or running shoes so that we could "Just Do It" as our favorite athletes do, and if their name is on the side, we'll spend entire paychecks on them. We've been searching for a label to replace the hated terms of Communism or Socialism as the utopia where we all share and nobody goes without, but they remain Boogie Men to fear, so we'll keep dishing out our hard-earned gold-backed dollars for health care that doesn't really take care of our health. I'll see you at the walk-in clinic and hope I get a good nurse practitioner.

HAVE A NICE DAY

In the early 70s, Philadelphian brothers Murray and Bernard Spain designed and sold bumper stickers and coffee mugs festooned with a yellow smiley face, which was created by commercial artist, Harvey Ball. Harvey was the first one to blow it, as he never applied for a trademark and was only paid a whopping $45 for it. The design came about when he was asked by an insurance company that had just merged with another insurance company to design something to alleviate the predictable low morale of the employees that naturally occurs when two insurance companies merge. The genius idea was to have the employees wear the smiley face buttons to remind them to smile while on the phone or in person with customers, because everyone needs to smile while taking out policies to enrich other people when they die. But the trick worked, which told us more about insurance company employees than the design itself. The buttons actually caught on outside the insurance biz and by 1971, more than 50 million buttons had been sold. Who can actually state what that says about the consumer taste in the 70s? Or just the 70s, period?

Originally, the slogan, *Have a Happy Day* became associated with the design, but the Spain Brothers altered that to the iconic, "Have a Nice Day." And somehow, the world began to import the design and its platitude.

It became intertwined in pop culture, first with the 1986 graphic novel *Watchmen*, as they corrupted the symbol as part of their villain Comedian look by having a blood splatter on the perennially grinning smiley face. Mel Gibson shot up a target with the smiley face image at a shooting range in 1987's *Lethal Weapon* and quipped to Danny Glover's Murtaugh for effect, "Have a Nice Day." Next came the film *Forrest Gump* in 1994, as a better origin story was told, having the eponymous idiot use the phrase after wiping his mud-splattered mug with the banana-yellow T-shirt a failing T-shirt hawker gave him to wipe the schmutz off. Professional wrestler Mick Foley used it as part of the title for his 1999, New York Times #1 best-selling autobiography, as it was one of his catchphrases for the Hannibal Lecter-inspired character, Mankind. In the late 90s to the 2010s, The Smiley Face Murder Theory espoused that a number of young men found dead in bodies of water across several mid-Atlantic states didn't actually drown but were the victims of either one or several different serial killers. The theory was developed after graffiti depicting the smiley face was discovered near the bodies of at least a dozen of the cases. So naturally, the murderers were dubbed The Smiley Face Killers and became a 2019 docuseries on the cable network, Oxygen. The irony should not be lost that the "Have a Nice Day" slogan became associated with a possible serial killer. And not to be outdone, a slasher film was made titled *The Smiley Face Killers,* directed by Tim Hunter, who helmed several *Breaking Bad* episodes. The film was written by Bret Easton Ellis—who had given us *American Psycho*, which actually makes for a great double feature when paired with *Mary Poppins* for the seriously mentally ill film buff. The order in which you watch them has been used as a key question in multiple neuro-psychological exams.

The phrase has since become part of the vox populi as many celebrities in varying fields have used it to convey the feelings in mostly sarcastic and biting manners:

"People always tell me 'Have a Nice Day.' What if I don't want to? What if I want to have a crappy day?"

—George Carlin

"In five billion years, the sun will expand and engulf our orbit. As the charred ember that was once Earth vaporizes. Have a nice day."

—Neil deGrasse Tyson

"White people scare the crap out of me. I have never been attacked by a black person, never been evicted by a black person, never had my security deposit ripped off by a black person, never been pulled over by a black cop, never been sold a lemon by a black car salesman, never had a black person deny me a bank loan, never had a black person bury my movie, and I've never heard a black person say, 'We're going to eliminate ten thousand jobs here—have a nice day!'"

—Michael Moore

"Just saying no prevents teenage pregnancy the way 'Have a nice Day' cures depression."

—Faye Wattleton

"When the world gets in my face, I say, 'Have a nice day.'"

—Jon Bon Jovi

So where has 50 years of telling each other to *Have a Nice Day* and showing a mutant smiley face gotten us? How did a delightful yellow smile and a bland but perfectly reasonable pleasantry become so corrupted into meaning the polar opposite of their original designs? Simple.

Human beings, and especially Americans, corrupt everything from overuse. Enjoy an occasional two-martini lunch? How about developing that—into sucking down an entire bottle of vodka, or binging through the 12-pack the moment we get home from work? Start a minor dalliance with heroin by joy-popping? Congratulations, you now have a full-throated addiction. Feel a little warm and fuzzy by wearing your delightful yellow shirt with a happy face and telling friends and strangers alike to have a nice day? Well, it morphed into a double-eyeball sinus headache every time you spot it. It became that incessant car alarm in the middle of the night that never gets shut off, and then does a three-part harmony with the passing ambulance and police car every time you hear it spoken. Taking that gestalt to it to its reductio ad absurdum now means the pursuit of happiness has become, "I will do all I can to prevent your pursuit of happiness, and while it doesn't make me happy, it fans the flames of my anger enough where I can at least feel slight pangs of pleasure by denying you yours. So up your political party that I don't identify with; immigrants from countries I don't admire; skin colors that don't reflect my own melanin; genders I don't understand and thus despise." And on and on it goes, until we have all developed nothing but disdain for the majority of the population that don't fit into our preferred categories.

If I can't have a nice day, I'll be damned if I'll allow anyone else to have one. And I will spend virtually all my time, energy and resources denying you that nice day that for decades. I spent many a moment glibly passing it along when I never really meant it, but now, damn you, I can't even muster the strength to utter it sarcastically. I will curse you to your face and pray for your unholy ruin! And don't think for a second that you can diffuse my anger by turning the other cheek, or trying to hug it out so we can all just get along. Screw that! No writing "Fat Man" or "Little Boy" on the atomic bombs we drop on your ass. One will say "Have a Nice Day" while the other will have the Smiley Face painted on it, and after I witness the rising mushroom cloud from the ashes of your mass incineration, then and only then will I even consider my day to be at least OK, provided that it isn't raining. Or a little chilly.

So *everyone* blew that. Virtually everyone on the planet has said, intimated or thought of conveying "have a nice day" to somebody, possibly even meaning it on occasion. But with repetition came subversion, and it described how the word *bad* eventually meant *good*. And the semiotics of Smiley Face soon projected our true feelings: eyebrows arched down, tongue sticking out, and the real feeling of "Have a Shitty Day" came vomiting out of all of us. So this one is on our collective soul.

CABLE TELEVISION

In 1976, inherited billboard magnate Ted Turner introduced what he coined as the first SuperStation. He had purchased a crappy, independent UHF station, WTCG in Atlanta, and then went into his Board of Directors meeting with a plastic model of a satellite and said that this was what they were going to use to get that signal to broadcast all over the United States. The Satcom II telecom satellite had been launched, and Turner discovered that leasing their transponders to upload and download a TV signal was relatively inexpensive, and he would then be able to get *Andy Griffith* reruns into millions of homes by having that signal go into various local and regional cable stations to distribute to their customers. Realizing that having original content would be even better than watching Barney Fife ad infinitum, Turner proceeded to buy up entities that could provide such content, starting with the National Wrestling Alliance's (NWA) Georgia Championship Wrestling, which he would redub World Championship Wrestling (WCW). He followed that up by purchasing perennial losers The Atlanta Braves baseball team and the Atlanta Hawks basketball team. The rechristened TBS became the second TV network to beam their signal via satellite, after Home Box Office (HBO), the first premium cable network, which began transmission in 1972.

So now, TV viewers could watch sports, wrestling, and a litany of early black and white TV shows, along with unedited movies, which stoked the likes of little Timmys everywhere whose hearts palpitated at the sight of real boobies and the sounds of words such as "fuck," "shit," and even "motherfucker" and the remaining seven words George Carlin once said you could never say on TV. WGN out of Chicago joined the satellite fray in 1978, adding the Cubs and White Sox as America's teams. And in 1979, WWOR out of Secaucus, New Jersey, began uplinking their signal to cable and satellite subscribers, getting their program national distribution.

But Ted Turner wasn't finished, not by a long shot. In 1980, he started CNN, the first 24-hour all-news cable network, and there was much laughter and finger-pointing and derisive comments about his manhood and probably some about his mother. But he was just warming up. He followed CNN up with Headline News, TNT, Cartoon Network, and just about any other niche network he could think of. If there was a block of programming he could buy, he created a network, and if there was a place where people accumulated and stared off into space for considerably long times, he installed monitors so they could watch CNN instead of people watch. Soon, people standing in line at airports, supermarkets, and bar restrooms were given consumer opportunities to watch what was once dubbed the Chicken Noodle Network.

In 1996, both Fox News and MSNBC premiered and the swamp of TV news was truly born. But things were just heating up.

U2 had their Zoo Tv tour in 1992 to satire the disparate TV viewing of the Gulf War, mass media, and *morning zoo* radio formats. Bruce Springsteen had a minor hit in 1992 with *57 Channels & Nothing On*, which seems so quaint now. Today, 57 channels is just the premium, minor-league baseball package. What they thought were insightful and satirical comments describing the sad state of TV content and our brainwashed viewing, while mildly amusing, didn't actually capture the true nature of the addiction. YouTube became the first streaming, video-sharing service in 2005. Netflix, which launched in 1997 to seemingly go after Blockbuster with their DVD-shipping rental program, gave away their ultimate agenda with their name (oh, and Blockbuster—

you actually *turned down* the opportunity to buy Netflix for 50 million in 2000! Maybe you would have continued their service or done what many mergers do: shut down the opposition, in which case we would still be successful in getting us to leave our domiciles in order to procure our evening's entertainment before becoming permanent squatters in our homes. Nice going!).

They were aiming to have movies (Flix) on the Internet (Net). And so they did, starting in 2010. Apple iTunes joined the media circus in 2005, and this is where things went: a gazillion streaming services that produce original content for varying prices, tiers, and premiums, making our cable bills long enough to carpet a modest three-bedroom home. Sure, you can eliminate basic cable and just go with streaming services, but to get what you really want, you end up with countless bundles, add-ons, and who knows what else just so you can get your fix of news, sports, original programs, and whatever else they can think of throwing at us. A typical conversation between two Generation Z or Millennials or whatever generation moniker we're on often goes something like this:

Gen Zer 1: Have you seen that new program on Hulu? *Organic Ninja Monkeys on the Supreme Court?*

Gen Zer 2: Why no, any good?

Gen Zer 1: Oops. They just cancelled it. But look, Youku just picked up a second season of *Flunkies.*

Gen Zer 2: Great, I love that show—but not as much as I love *Figgy Pudding* on iQIYI.

Gen Zer 1: Did you see where Peacock is going to have a 36-hour marathon of *Pickles and Clam Shells?*

Gen Zer 2: Wait, I thought they only made one episode of that show?

Gen Zer 1: They did. So we get to binge-watch that show for 36 hours straight. Mind blown!

TBS

SUPERSTATION

So between Covid and the combo of cable TV and streaming services, we have basically eliminated all reasons to leave the house. We've killed the mall, and movie theaters and restaurants that don't deliver. Everything we need can be delivered through Amazon and Uber Eats or distributed to us on our entertainment systems, laptops and iPhones. All actual face-to-face contact is a thing of the past. We're so much closer to making Woody Allen's *Sleeper*'s orgasmatron not just a reality, but a necessity. Maybe this was all actually concocted by Woody Allen in the first place. The way to escape certain death is to never actually be alive.

NORMAN GREENBAUM

Norman Greenbaum is your dentist, your accountant, your lawyer, your high school science teacher, your gynecologist. Norman Greenbaum is *not* the name of the writer/performer of the greatest one-hit wonder of all time. You're not an orthodox Jew, growing up in the ethnic suburb of Malden, MA (my granddad delivered him), performing as a folk and a jug band artist and then, somehow, creating "Spirit in the Sky." That just doesn't happen.

Only it did.

From the opening, dirty, fuzz guitar riff, and then the syncopated hand claps, followed by the most ironic yet uplifting lyrics mentioning Jesus, "Spirit in the Sky" did everything you want a song to do, including forcing you to remember the name: Norman Greenbaum. Try and pull out the names of those who sang "Band of Gold" or "Tighter and Tighter" or even "Mambo No. 5." They might make great *Jeopardy* questions one day.

OK, technically, Greenbaum had two other, minor hits: "Canned Ham," which reached number 46 in 1970, and "The Eggplant that Ate Chicago," from his Dr. West's Medicine Show Jug Band, that charted (barely) in 1967. But those were the more typical novelty hits, like "They're Coming to Take Me Away," or "Monster Mash," you know, the type that got played on the *Dr. Demento* radio show. "Spirit in the Sky" sold 2 million copies in 1969 and 1970 and hit number one all over the world. Fifty films featured the song on its soundtrack, including

Apollo 13, Oceans 11, The Longest Yard, Miami Blues, Wayne's World II, Remember the Titans, and *Gonzo.* William Shatner covered it!

The word "die" is mentioned nine times. Nine! And we're promised nothing. We're gonna get a *recommendation* to the "Spirit in the Sky." It's like LinkedIn. So an Orthodox Jew, playing some of the greatest, dirty, fuzzbox guitar, singing about Jesus and where we go after we shuffle off this mortal coil (hint—it's the *best*) blew it...or did we?

This one is on all of us.

Just like "Just Do It," the uplifting message, massive hook-laden song promises us nothing but inspires us to not fear the biggest bummer, but to embrace it. So it's more hope for the hopeless, and who needs that? I don't need a catchy tune in my head that makes me sing along and feel good when I know it's all just a load of crap. Life sucks and then you die, and you're not going to see the "Spirit in the Sky." Give me Bloodrock's "DOA" every time.

Greenbaum wrote the song in 15 minutes, inspired by a greeting card that had the eponymous title on it. And Hopi Indians—of course it would be a tribe called Hopi. He claimed that the rest of his inspiration came from Porter Waggoner gospel songs and western movies with cowboys getting killed by Indians and wanting to die with their boots on. I was hoping for more of a Jim Morrison-type story about a horrible car accident (Norman Greenbaum was in a very bad one, but many years later) with Indians bleeding and dying on the road as he watched their spirits ascend into the heavens, which greatly impacted his *fragile, eggshell mind.* Turns out he just watched a lot of John Wayne flicks, listened to Gospel/country, watched syndicated TV shows, saw a greeting card, and wrote the greatest song ever.

Screw it, the entire concept is perfect—the song, the lyrics, the origin, everything. Maybe this time, we all get a pass. Maybe Dennis Hopper's Billy's initial reaction, "We did it," wasn't off after all. So, have a shot of "Tequila" so as not cry "96 Tears" which could cause you to Wipeout" as you get "Hooked on a Feeling" thinking about an "Afternoon Delight" followed by "Walking on Sunshine" and "I'm Gonna Be 500 Miles" so I'll call you at "867-5309" because "I'm Too Sexy," isn't that right, "Sugar Sugar?"

THE NATIONAL ENQUIRER

It's not really counterintuitive to put any blame on *The National Enquirer* for dumbing down America. It actually wasn't always that way. When they began, their goal was actually to scare the crap out of America with headlines such as, "I Cut Out Her Heart and Stomped On It" (1963), or "Mom Boiled Her Baby and Ate Her" (1962). The Enquirer we have come to know and loathe (well, some of us) is more well known for "Hillary Clinton Adopts Alien Baby" or "Charlie Sheen Aids Cover Up." They picked up on the motherload in 1977 with Elvis's death and the plethora of ensuing headlines detailing both his decadent lifestyle of sex, drugs, and peanut-butter-and-banana sandwiches, eaten while assassinating innocent television sets. But their real evil ways came about when they totally changed the structure of how magazines like theirs could be sold: at the supermarket checkout.

They actually weren't the first magazine to do so. That honor goes to *Family Circle* and *Woman's Day* in 1971. But the genius of *The National Enquirer* was to implement a program so nefarious that similar programs in other entertainment businesses made it illegal. In radio, paying DJs to play your record was known as payola or pay-to-play, and it's what destroyed rock and roll legend Alan Freed. But *The National Enquirer* was much more devious by coming up with a name that totally hid the notion that what they were doing was a grift, or graft, or grift graft. They named their program RDA for Retail Display Allowance.

NATIONAL
ENQUIRER

Supermarkets, bookstores, and newsstands pay distributors for the magazines they sell. They then rip off the covers and return the unsold back to the distributors to get full credit. Often, they never even put a title out if they felt that it was a POS and just ripped off the covers and sent them back, all the while insisting that they put them out on display as part of their contractual obligation. But The Enquirer offered the supermarkets a percentage of the sale of each magazine, over and above the contracted percentage. This was in addition to the cost they incurred as they were the ones responsible for actually installing all the wire racks at the checkouts for the magazine display. And mama mia, did the supermarkets make bank. They began charging additional fees for rack position. If you were in the top right corner of the rack, you would have to pay an arm and a leg for the honor. This set off a huge bidding war among the magazines vying for the best positions. The *Enquirer* and their competitors were actually the first pop-up ads and for that, there should be a nice place in hell reserved for them.

Just as we are locked onto our computer screens and paying through the nose for ad blockers to reduce the clutter of insurance pop-ups from getting any eyeball time, so were the traditional housewives locked in at the checkout line while Gladys, mother of five, was doing her weekly shopping and loading up the conveyor belt with a pile that could occupy serious space at today's Walmart. She and her counterparts were stuck in that space, eyes glazing over with nowhere to look except the tantalizing headlines staring out at them from the magazine checkout rack. They unconsciously picked up the one with the most salacious headline and started thumbing through it as their massive order was filling the paper bags that inevitably would cause her eggs to break prior to reaching her back door due to the 10-pound tin of Spam sitting on top of them. They would sigh and flip the magazine onto the waning pile of food to finish the article about Elizabeth Taylor's upcoming wedding to a shaved, headless ape. Those poor women read countless articles about aliens, political scandals, and celebrity screwups, turning their *Feminine Mystique* into a pile of oatmeal while they were at their most vulnerable. The jig should have been up when *The Enquirer* reported that Cher had three months to live, because alien babies on Mars readying for an attack on Earth were more believable than that.

That was the first crack, the first time children saw Mom's credibility as an adult figure capable of rearing children into functional adults took a serious hit. She would come home with an armful of bird-cage lining as *The National Enquirer, The Weekly World News, Cosmopolitan,* and possibly *Guns and Ammo*, then lecture her kids about how comic books were filling their heads with garbage, folderol, and nonsense. As we sprouted into teens, they turned their leery eyes on us when they noticed us flipping through our collections of *Mad Magazine* and *National Lampoon,* beating their chests with the notion of their failure as parents, which lasted but a moment as they quickly turned to see if they could save their failing marriages by serving Dad's dinner of beef stroganoff in the nude (their marriages *were* failing, as the dads were preoccupied with their own tumult of balancing a dead-end job, a needy mistress, and a slow descent into alcoholism and despair). *National Lampoon* excoriated the entire concept of Mom's parenting skills with the scathing parody issue dubbed "Negligent Mother," whose cover featured two women having a cheerful gabfest over the wooden property fence as junior was floating face down in the kiddie pool in the background. The Newtonian response to that produced helicopter parents who would never be accused of being negligent and would have preferred keeping their children in their womb for life, if there was room.

So a brilliant idea from the crappiest magazines ever helped blow it for generations of children, marriages, and the societal glue that has been pecked at measurably since 1969. And in other news, the celebrity gossip website, TMZ, broke the story that King of Pop Michael Jackson died from a potpourri of drugs that stopped his heart in 2009.

But that was hardly surprising, as they had been camped out for decades trying to catch Macaulay Culkin or some other former child star leaving Neverland Ranch under cover of night, for a classic gotcha journalism moment.

IT'S THE END OF THE WORLD AS WE KNOW IT (I FEEL FINE)

R.E.M released that in 1987, which name-checks a lot of people,-mostly people with the name Leonard or Lenny. It does mention Trump, in what was their most Nostradamus-like stanza:

Team by team reporters baffled, trump, tethered crop
Look at that low plane! Fine, then
Uh oh, overflow, population, Common Food
But it'll do. Save yourself, serve yourself
World serves its own needs, listen to your heart bleed
Tell me with the rapture and the reverent in the right, right
You vitriolic, patriotic, slam, fight, bright light
Feeling pretty psyched

But the song was mostly a bunch of strung-together words, sung as gibberish in singer Michael Stipe's special brand of mumbling. Still, they were on to something. The end of the world had a ton of predictions in the time-post *Easy Rider*, and the doom and gloom kept rocking the airwaves, internet and anyplace where Earthlings can learn of their predictable, ultimate demise.

Y2K was the perfect place to start, as it was a technological doomsday clock that had virtually everyone on the planet stockpiling

Depends for January 1, 2000. Yes, Y2K, the infamous "millennium bug," was expected to cause global chaos, with fears that airplanes would fall out of the sky and missiles would fire by accident, all simply by the hypothetical resetting of dates on computers at the stroke of midnight on 1 January 2000.

By now, the Internet is known for its ability to spread hoaxes and prompt unfounded fear, but Y2K was one of the earliest examples of this. Songs like "Y2K - The Bug is Coming" by the band Y2K (a supergroup featuring Ian Dury, Jim-Bob from Carter the Unstoppable Sex Machine, and Fuzz Townshend) did little to diffuse the situation.

But in the end, nothing happened, and the world continued as it was before. There were two ways to look at the millennium bug: one is that it was largely a fuss about nothing—fear mongering from people who should really have known better. The other is that it really was a potential problem, avoided only thanks to the hard work of technicians finding a way around it.

However, that's not to say we haven't been dogged by such problems ever since. A slightly less catastrophic instance came in 2014 when PSY's *Gangnam Style* exceeded YouTube's view limit, breaking the site's view counter in doing so. The massive hit (and its much-parodied video) has since led to the video site to up its maximum view count to 9,223,372,036,854,775,808, or just over nine quintillion. Correct at the time of publishing, we've not seen a video reach nine quintillion views just yet. But someone will eventually beat that number on TikTok, and then we can all go back to our 1960s underground nuclear bunkers again, thank goodness. We could all use a blast from the past.

Herbert Armstrong was one of the first televangelists to give a specific date for the end of the world. He made two predictions prior to 1969 on radio, but continued his revisions to include 1972 and 1975. The fourth time wasn't the charm. Perennial national embarrassment Pat Robertson predicted on his show that the End of the World would occur in 1982, and when that blew up in his face, he tried again, but in book form. His 1990 book, *The New Millennium*, marked our calendars for April 29, 2007. Wrong again. He spends most of his time now on his *700 Club* TV show, waxing total gibberish about Republican politics and his version of morality. He has become the poster child for the corrupt lack of separation between church and mental state.

Harold Camping might have been the most interesting of all the failed televangelists and predictors of our collective shuffling-off veil of tears. His preachings were often in total contradiction to what most of the evangelicals taught regarding the literal teachings of the Old and New Testament, the age of the Earth, and other Biblical events. In 1992, Camping published a book titled *1994?* where he predicted Christ's return on September 6, 1994 and The Rapture on May 21, 2011, with the End of the World happening on October 21, 2011. After his prognostications proved wrong again and again, his following dwindled down to a major league baseball-roster size of 25. Now Camping wasn't completely wrong, as actor Jackson Pickney was awarded $487,000 from being blinded by Jean-Claude Van Damme while making the film, *Cyborg* on September 6, 1994 and May 21, 2011 was the running of 136th Preakness, with Jesús Castañón aboard Shackleford, who won in 1:56.47. Now ,on October 21, 2011, President Obama announced troop withdrawal from Iraq, so we can probably call that last prediction a push. Damn, Camping came so close. It's just a matter of interpretation.

Of course, there were many others on the wrong side of their predictions. Jack Van Impe and his lovely wife, Rexella, often did their best Magic 8 Ball on their half-hour TV show, *Van Impe Presents,* which actually had a global audience. His sermons were often apocalyptic, warning of the end times due to war with Russia, homosexuality, the merger of Christianity and Islam (Chrislam, he called it), and rooting for the New York Jets.

But the best of the lot, the Tom Brady of charismatic soothsayers of doom, had to be Jonathan Cahn, the son of Holocaust survivors who transformed into an end-of-times evangelist. He studied Nostradamus, and the Virginia psychic, Edgar Cayce. He became a hippie-like preacher, and his *are-you-kidding-me* theories about ancient astronauts and other sermons have been uploaded onto social media platforms like YouTube and Facebook. He has since become an author, with his first book, *The Paradigm,* tying his prophetic teachings to the election of Donald J. Trump. And to that end, he often makes appearances with the likes of Michelle Bachmann, Mike Huckabee, and that Punxsutawney Phil of prognostications, Mike Lindell.

Cahn was predicting "The End" before his conversion to "Trump as The Chosen One," as he did in 2015. He brushed off his blowing-of-that-one by saying he always used disclaimers and "you just can't put God in a box." Yes, when you look in your rearview mirror, the End of Times might actually be further than it appears. Or is it farther? Hard to predict.

So this one is easy: the clown car of prophets blew it because, well, they haven't gotten it right yet, and they have tried, literally, for centuries. But eventually, like a broken watch, one of them will get it right. Of course, neither the predictor nor the rest of us sheeples will be able to hear his

proclamation of *"told ya,"* as that's what being right would mean. And then it's only a hop, skip, and a jump before one of them claims the Apocalypse was rigged, and it actually happened but for some interference from a combination of Italian satellites and the Antichrist's visa not being properly issued from the Left-Wing Radicals in the Underworld, it failed to occur. We blew it, because a frightening amount of people among us still believe that nonsense. And always will. Until the End.

ARNOLD SCHWARZENEGGER

You can actually trace the evolution of health and fitness in America by looking at the progression of Arnold Schwarzenegger's acting career.

In 1970, Arnold had his first role in the accidental comedy, *Hercules in New York*. Billed as Arnold Strong, *HINY* had the misfortune, or incredible foresight, to have Arnold as Hercules sent to New York, where he finds True Love and a career as a bodybuilder. Riding around Central Park with his date, Arnold noticed a bear, because bears in Central Park were an incredible nuisance in the 70s. He leapt from his chariot to engage in mortal combat with the bear, who was so obviously a man in a bear suit that one hoped that this film's producers actually intended it to be a comedy, that is if they ever wanted to work in the Biz again. Another giveaway was the fact that the other famous Arnold, Arnold Stang, had a prominent role. Dueling Arnolds simply don't work in film; it's a proven fact. Health clubs at that time were seen much like Arnold was in the film: a joke to be ignored. As ticket buyers stayed away from *Hercules in New York* in droves, so did personal health enthusiasts stay away from the dying remnants of health club chains such as Vic Tanny and even TV star Jack LaLanne's gyms, choosing instead to go with fat loss scams such as Dexatrim which could cause seizures and hypertensive crises. Besides, protesting the Vietnam War and marching for Women's and Civil Rights proved to be a great cardio workout. In addition to the marches, fights with

police caused a multitude of people to flee for their lives, possibly being one of the igniters of the jogging craze that ensued. Monkee flee, monkee do.

1973 saw Arnold in the fantastic Robert Altman film, *The Long Goodbye*, which starred Elliot Gould as a sort of zen Philip Marlowe. Arnold was an uncredited hired goon in a scene where he mercifully had no lines (his original dialogue in *Hercules in New York* was dubbed, but so was Mel Gibson's from *Mad Max,* so Arnold had nothing to feel bad about other than his acting). Arnold perfectly involved the stereotype—the large, muscular man who frequented the stinky, sweaty clubs with the broken machines and rotting weights and didn't talk much about his obsession as the population at large ensured that it wasn't shared amongst polite society. In his 1974 appearance in *Happy Anniversary and Goodbye,* Arnold fared a little better as he even exchanged dialogue with Lucille Ball and Art Carney, but it didn't go march further than him blurting out "I am Rico," and then making a thinly veiled double entendre joke about the state of undress Lucy was in for her impending workout. And so it went as the first utterance you might get out of the early-70s weightlifter—perhaps their name and the fact that they do go to whatever sweatshop gym was around to pick things up and put them down—but not much more than that.

Arnold finally got a role where he could play himself—sort of. In

Bob Rafelson's 1976 film *Stay Hungry,* Arnold was Joe Santos, Mr. Austria training for the Mr. Universe contest in a gym that was being targeted to be acquired by a shady businessman who really wanted to tear it down and build a high-rise. They used Jeff Bridges as a front and Arnold was often himself, as in one scene, where he wore a Batman outfit while doing bicep curls in the gym because, as in real life, he enjoyed freaking people out and shaking things up for personal amusement. He also played fiddle in a country and bluegrass outfit and for those reasons, he was awarded a Golden Globe for Best Movie Debut, meaning that The Hollywood Foreign Press Association intentionally ignored Arnold's initial starring role in his *Hercules Fights a Fake Bear in Central Park* movie. So gyms and fitness were still being seen just as Arnold was: a joke, but at least an interesting one. He was permitted to tell the occasional joke instead of just being the butt of one. It seemed that health clubs and fitness in America wasn't destined for the scrap heap of history.

Or maybe it was.

1977 featured Arnold guest-starring in an Episode of *The Streets of San Francisco,* where he played a bodybuilder continually being laughed at by women about his physique. In the first depiction of 'roid rage on celluloid, he murdered them after being duped into posing. Big mistake. Arnold was educating us about the secrets behind the giant, hulking musclemen and the adverse effects of becoming a side of beef, and it was funny right up to the point where you get stomped on as a result of the infusion of Dianabol in a jacked-out freak. We all turned a collective side-eye to the burgeoning health and fitness industry as we were appalled by their representatives and had zero interest in emulating them, unless you were 12 and reading the Charles Atlas ad in a comic book, showing how Mac was turned into a Man. Kids were sending away for his free book, but adults avoided buying gym memberships. But the streets were free, and so running/jogging started getting popular.

It didn't end well, as that so-called healthy lifestyle change known as "running at a medium pace while wearing ridiculously short shorts" blew up into a full-force trend, thanks to Jim Fixx's book, *The Complete Book of Running*, which combined the popularity of running with new age, self-help propaganda. Fixx was an overweight, heavy smoker who took up jogging as a way to get healthy, and when it worked, he parlayed his routine into a revenue stream as he promised others how they could gain from the physical and psychological benefits of sort-of running and following pseudo, 12-step twaddle. It was so successful that President Jimmy Carter took it jogging in 1979 to counteract the perception that he was weak in dealing with Ronald Reagan. Unfortunately, that backfired when he collapsed in the middle of a 10K race, thus clearing the path to Reagan's win.

That lost race precipitated a policy of ignoring a killer virus when those in power decided that those unlucky enough to contract the virus and die were actually people deserving of their fate. We all know where that attitude got us, both then and in today's blewdom hellscape. Not too ironically, Fixx died at the age of 52 in 1984 from a heart attack...while running. One of his teachings from his books was to listen to your bodies and not doctors, and if you believe you can push through the pain, you should. We learned two things from Arnold's role in *TSOSF*: that exercise can make you want to kill others, and that exercise itself can kill you. Or homophobic politicians can kill you. And idiots, idiots can kill you. Arnold's Hollywood career and the fitness industry left us with mixed messages in the 70s and beyond.

In 1982, Arnold was cast as *Conan the Barbarian*, a fearless, invincible fighter who gave us the iconic answer to what is best in life: "To crush your enemies. To have them driven before you and to hear the lamentations of the women!"

But the women weren't so into the whole "lamentation" thing. In 1982, Jane Fonda released her first workout tape, and suddenly women from all over the country were putting on their leggings, getting down on the mat, and cardioing their way to a svelte fitness the men couldn't even begin to imagine (but often did, in the shower). And in the latter part of 1981, Olivia Newton John's *Let's Get Physical* came out, so there was double incentive for the ladies to get in shape and fight our entire Conan fetish. *Time Magazine's* November 1981 cover story was about *The Fitness Craze; America Shapes Up.* And with the previously mentioned "Just Do It," America was finally fighting the flab—or at least trying. Not an easy thing to do when McDonald's was Super Sizing everything. But Arnold and the majority cast of glistening, muscled bodies, both male and female, helped lead the way. American Exceptionalism was finally producing Exceptional Americans.

1984 and '85 gave us *Conan The Destroyer, Commando, Red Sonja,* and of course, *The Terminator.* Arnold's pecs, biceps, latissimus dorsi, and even his gluteus maximus were on display in a smorgasbord of the flesh. Health clubs became the new singles bar, and we downed protein shakes and smoothies as our budget for supplements reached our former drug and alcohol expenditures (but offering a lot less fun). Even the elderly among us were *Sweatin' to the Oldies* and buying home gyms or little devices hawked by the likes of Body By Jake and the ponytailed Tony Little. And then in 1987, Arnold came out with *Predator*, where the entire cast was on the juice. It featured two future Governors in Jesse "The Body" Ventura and Arnold himself. It also had Rocky's Apollo Creed and a gaggle of well-oiled and muscled macho men. Ventura actually had the line of the film, with, "I ain't got time to bleed," the perfect quote to accompany "no pain, no gain." He followed that up with *The Running Man,* whose title even informed us of the need to work out. Even his 1988 comedy *Twins* reminded us of the differences between the stud (Arnold) and The Dud (Danny DeVito), and we all know who we wanted to look like.

Arnold's output in the 90s consisted of a couple of *Terminator* sequels, plus *Total Recall* and *Kindergarten Cop.* He's still a badass, but the formula was wearing thin for the national fitness obsession, as the 90s produced The Thighmaster, ellipticals, the women's health club chain Curves, spin classes, the NordicTrack and Eight-Minute Abs.

By the 2000s, Arnold was getting a little long in the tooth—but not for politics, as the recall of Democratic Governor Gray Davis led to a man who could never lose his accent being elected Governor of California, foreshadowing another California governor recall specifically over the incumbent's position on a public health crisis, with Arnold weighing in on the stupidity of people choosing not to get vaccinated or wear masks. And this was where we all blew it. Our health icons age, and we totally forget why they inspired us in the first place, and people like Reagan and Trump made it OK to deny public health and science if many people on the losing end of a virus or pandemic are people that many among us just don't like. Maybe Arnold needs to do a remake of *Contagion* or *Outbreak*.

All we have these days in the macho, super fit canon are The Rock and John Cena, who both came out of the fake professional wrestling biz. So they can be box office boffo, but they aren't inspiring us to hit the weights, especially when gyms became incubators for doom and despair, catching something on things other than toilet seats. Many people are getting their food delivered, and regardless of if the pizza is vegan, you're still going to fluff up nicely. Now our young, male actors are the likes of Timothée Chalamet, Tom Holland, Nic Robinson, and Noah Schnapp—heartthrobs all, but not busting out of their XXL T-shirts, smashing bullies in the face and telling them it's their turn to "dry up and blow away." If we still had Conan the Barbarian's Arnold telling us to vax and mask up, you can damn well be sure we would be. But his relevance has waned and with that, his impact on public opinion and action. We seem doomed to repeat the gaffes of the 70s and 80s. We're a sequel no one wants a ticket for.

THE SOCIAL NETWORK

This refers to the 2008 film by David Fincher, not the actual Social Media Capitalist Communication Conglomerate we all have ceded our souls to—although it's impossible to describe one without the other, especially within the confines of blowing it. You can't get a better combination of revenge theorists than director David Fincher and screenwriter Aaron Sorkin, who, combined, have brought us the revenge tales of a cop who killed the psychopath who murdered his wife; the split-personality sociopath whose alter ego helped enact revenge on all those whose ignorance devolved into a series of imagined slights; and the navy lawyer who had to prove that he wasn't just a man with both courtroom and daddy issues.

The Social Network premiered on October 1, 2010, just a mere six years after Facebook's actual humble beginnings in a Harvard dorm room. The movie was basically an entire revenge plot, as Mark Zuckerberg was shown as motivated through his misogynist feelings stemming from a breakup in the first scene; Sean Parker's angst towards the venture capitalists, board directors and music business icons who relentlessly pursued and humiliated him as a result of his creating Napster and other social media startups; and Eduardo Saverin and the Winklevoss twins, whose fucking-over by Zuckerberg would suffice to fuel anyone's deep dive into the world of legal remedy. It added to the class battle of the WASPS vs the Jews in the social hierarchy of Harvard's exclusive clubs, which gave rise to the conclusion that virtually everyone in the film was an asshole, and all it asked us to do was identify with the one asshole we found the least objectionable.

Only six years into the revolution that Facebook caused, *The Social Network* never got into the role Facebook would play as a petri dish for disinformation, political manipulation, conspiracy theories, extremist groups, online bullying, and the ethics (or lack thereof) for algorithms designed specifically to mine all our data for targeted advertising, which became the core of Facebook's billion-dollar revenue streams. But levying the charge of the unenlightened toward the Founders would be as unfair as blaming the Wright Brothers for not anticipating that bombs would one day fall from their invention.

In 1932, British scientists had succeeded in splitting the atom for the first time by artificial means, although some believed it couldn't produce huge amounts of energy. But the same year, the Hungarian emigre physicist Leo Szilard read *The World Set Free,* by H.G. Wells, who predicted that we would one day see a weapon created of unimaginable power and destructive force. Szilard announced his belief that the splitting of the atom could produce vast energy, but that "vast energy" didn't immediately coalesce into the idea of atomic bombs. The argument as to how much responsibility inventors and entrepreneurs should be responsible for the usage of their creations, both intended and unintended, doesn't apply when the inventor of an application corrupts his own work into something he personally argued against, as Zuckerberg had.

The film's Zuckerberg was all barely restrained anger, irritability, and awkwardness as he tried to navigate the maze of college connection, both real and online. Today, those traits would ironically be considered the classic pattern of an internet troll, and the beginning of the film does have him trolling his recent breakup by lambasting her online via his drunkenly written blog. Saverin was the model for the online presence who would one day brag about his five thousand friends as he got punched by Harvard's most prestigious and exclusive final club, while Zuckerberg seethed with jealousy as no one liked or commented on his post.

In the end, all of the geeks won to some degree. Zuckerberg became the youngest billionaire on the planet, even if his final scene was being told by one of his lawyers, "You're not an asshole, Mark. You're just trying so hard to be," right before showing him in an endless loop refreshing his Facebook page after sending a friend request to his ex-girlfriend from the film's opening scene (and she also called him an asshole, to complete that loop). Eduardo Saverin and The Winklevoss Twins (referred to by Zuckerberg as The Winklevii) had received huge cash settlements from Zuckerberg—the Winklevii to the tune of sixty-five million and Saverin an undisclosed amount, which one must assume dwarfed the piddly couch cushions amount awarded to Tyler and Cameron.

But the film, unimpeachably, got one massive fact incredibly right. Zuckerberg's jumping-off point for creating Facebook was building the site FaceMash, which showed off his impressive abilities of hacking and coding, as well as his understanding of how to break a system at the world's most prestigious university. But what he actually excelled at was finding out what would motivate people to both look at his site and then share it, as that's the algorithm that turned a mean-spirited prank into a massive internet traffic jam that crashed the system and got the attention of the school's administration board and his fellow students. It was implied just how addictive an online presence could eventually be. Getting applauded or dissed on social media builds up a tolerance for the feelings, not unlike how drugs and alcohol are pressed into the addiction center of our brains. Over time, we require more of the drug to achieve the wanted effect.

With all of its inaccuracies regarding the main characters, *The Social Network* DID correctly predict the net effect of the platform's concept, and that would be the more time we spend digitally connecting, the more alone and isolated we become.

So we all fucking blew it, all three billion of us—which doesn't include the numbers on Instagram, Twitter, Snapchat, TikTok, and whatever evil social media incarnation is next developed and released as a hoax over a public that shouldn't be as unsuspecting as we once were.

the social network

The film continues to inspire legions of programmers and coders to make the Next Big Thing so they too can make, as Justin Timberlake's Sean Parker exclaimed, "a billion dollars" with matching business cards that read "I'm CEO, Bitch!" It's hard for any of us to claim victimhood anymore. We know what the digital world can do, has done, and will continue to do. Yet we are basically helpless to not go online; we can't avoid it any more than we could avoid jumping into mud puddles when we were really little. It's silly, juvenile, and leaves us all messy, which was always the point of jumping. Whatever negative interactions we received from parents and friends due to our online use paled from the instant satisfaction we get—or at least believe we get—from anything that artificial, superficial site posits as positive reactions. Or worse, when we felt the snarky superiority by trashing another person's post, thread, or comment with our *research* on a topic—jwhich consisted of Googling and reading the first link that showed up from our carefully worded question, guaranteed to find us the link that validated whatever opinion we had in order to make our point and raise our arms into a victory V. The line from the film might have been best spoken by the actor playing Larry Summers, the President at Harvard University:

"Well, the darkness is the absence of light, and the stupidity in that instance was the absence of me."

KNEES

"Be kind to your knees
You'll miss them when they're gone"
"Everybody's Free (To Wear Sunscreen)"
      —Baz Lurhmann (released March 9, 1999)

Aussie filmmaker Baz Luhrmann released this novelty song as a graduation speech to the class of 1997. He took it from an essay written by Pulitzer Prize-winning Chicago Tribune columnist, Mary Schmich. It was falsely attributed as an MIT graduation speech by writer Kurt Vonnegut. The spoken word piece reached #1 in many territories and hit #24 in Billboard for the US. There was lots of good advice, but for many, the knees might have been the best.

Many an athlete has seen his or her career cut short by knee injuries. Tearing your ACL, MCL, or meniscus was referred to as blowing out your knee, and it played heavily into the shortened careers of Bobby Orr, Gayle Sayers, Terrell Davis, Tiger Woods, Daunte Culpepper—it is an endless list. Knee injuries used to require extensive surgery, where a C-flap incision was made to expose the entire knee. But thanks to the development of arthroscopic surgery, many athletes nowadays return to compete at the same skill level they had prior to the injury. The progress made in fiber optics in the 70s and 80s was the breakthrough needed to enable the procedure to rehabilitate athletes from a form of

surgery that had actually been around since 1806. But there is one ath-lete whose career ended due to a knee *event*, and not an actual injury: Colin Kaepernick.

Kaepernick had been active on social media with commentary regarding the slew of fatal police shootings of Black men. During a preseason game in 2016, Kapernick sat instead of standing while the Star-Spangled Banner played. A reporter noticed it, and when asked why, Kaepernick responded:

"I am not going to stand up to show pride in a flag for a country that oppresses Black people and people of color. To me, this is bigger than football and it would be selfish on my part to look the other way. There are bodies in the street and people getting paid leave and getting away with murder."

Kaepernick's protest didn't gain much attention though, it being the preseason and he not being active due to injuries. In the fourth pre-season game, Kaepernick kneeled during the National Anthem, after he had a conversation with former NFL player and US Army Green Beret, Nate Boyer who suggested that kneeling would be considered more respectful to the military rather than sitting, as it was the tradition to kneel at a fallen soldier's grave. After all, kneeling has a long history of a gesture of respect. One knelt to receive knighthood in the days of King Arthur. The classic method of seeking your life partner to enter into marriage was to kneel while asking for their hand. Both Old and New Testament stories have kneeling as a sign of deference. Jesus knelt as part of the suffering and struggle he endured at Gethsemane on the eve of his crucifixion, with his posture serving as a sign of anguish as well as a mark of his true faithfulness. Kaepernick could have chosen to give a middle finger salute instead of kneeling.

As a result of his actions, Colin Kaepernick was effectively boycotted by NFL teams. He never received even a single workout to see if he could even back up a team's starting quarterback, never mind starting in a league rife with injuries. More galling was the fact that he had taken his former team, the San Francisco 49rs, to the Super Bowl. Kaepernick's knee *injury* put him in a similar situation to Muhammed Ali being stripped of his boxing heavyweight championship titles for being a conscientious objector to the Vietnam War. Kaepernick even earned him the insult by then-President Trump as a "son of a bitch" for his actions. His lawsuit against the NFL for colluding with team owners was settled by the league for an undisclosed sum.

So what might have happened if the NFL, team owners, fans, and the general public all embraced what Kaepernick was trying to do—call attention to an unjust matter that had been festering in our midst the moment slavery was supposedly abolished, and actually attempt to solve the problem? As with any disease, be it alcoholism or discrimination, it has to be recognized by both the individual and the collective before real change can happen. Yes, after George Floyd's murder, there seemed to be a tipping point where not only Americans protested en masse and demanded changes be made to fix the problem, and not just give platitudes and say a *Seinfeldian* "that's a shame," but people all over the world participated in protests, proving that this was not just an American problem. The world actually joined in with a collective admittance to the concept of blowing it. But it's what we do. We have a marvelous habit of tearing down our athletic heroes while they are in the midst of their struggles, at the time they need us the most, such as Fritz Pollard (the first Black NFL quarterback), Jim Thorpe, Jesse Owens, Jackie Robinson, Tommie Smith, John Carlos, The Black 14 University of Wyoming football players, The Syracuse Eight (who were actually nine but we didn't even get that right), Arthur Ashe, Bill Russell, Charlie Sifford, and Willie O'Ree, all of whom suffered from racism either due to their acts of protest or by the crime of playing sports while being Black. We blew it in one way or another with each and every one of them and a whole lot more. And for that, we all deserve a collective Tonya Harding blow to the kneecap.

YOGURT AND GRANOLA

It took a lot of guts for someone thinking that a semisolid food prepared from milk fermented with bacteria and having fruit mixed in was not only a good idea, but something you could successfully market to the average American consumer. By 1976 most supermarkets carried forty different types of yogurts—in three sizes, no less. In 1977, Dannon's famous "Georgians over 100" ad catapulted the industry to stratospheric heights with its depiction of really old people in the Soviet Bloc chopping wood and hoeing the sauerkraut fields. Georgians apparently do like yogurt, especially as a sunscreen (that must have made Baz Luhrmann happy) and for first-degree burns. What the campaign didn't show us was how most of those Georgians were screaming "kill me now" for having to chop wood and hoe the sauerkraut fields long past the age of Medicare (or whatever it's called in Georgia).

In 1978, Boston-based Brigham's Ice Cream Shoppes developed and packaged the first frozen yogurt, with the gag-reflex-stimulating name of Humphreez Yogart. TCBY took the baton from Brigham's and in 1981, opened their first frozen yogurt shop. By 1984, there were over 100 frozen yogurt chains nationwide. By 1986, we were devouring this germ-infested treat to the tune of $25 million in annual sales. Yup, Americans are the tourists of the food industry. We have proven, time and time again, that we will swallow almost anything, smiling for the camera while doing it.

Today's trend is the probiotic yogurt, which often targets women as their primary niche market. And why not? Just imply that ingesting this swill will stop ladies from farting like a buffalo on that romantic first date where you attempt to make her dinner, ending with a faked, homemade dessert of the latest in probiotic, wind-breaking-preventative yogurt. With fruit.

But the song *We Won't Get Fooled Again* doesn't apply to us here. Because for a probiotic to actually work in our tummy-tums, it has to follow some strict rules:

It must contain soil-based probiotics and be shelf-stable. Appetite stimulated, yet?

It has to have a high CFU count from at least 40 billion to 75 billion per serving and have at least 18 different strains. For you normal people who don't know what a CFU is, it stands for Colony Forming Units, which tells you how many good bacteria are able to divide themselves up and actually form a colony. Personally, they should just shorten the acronym to FU, as it seems more appropriate.

Oh, those different strains of probiotics it must contain? Dig some

of the names of those strains and then decide how quickly you want those as part of your meal: Bacillus coagulans, Lactobacillus acidophilus, Bifidobacterium, and Streptococcus thermophilus. Just try to suppress the "Mmm-mmm, good" from leaving your lips.

But do they work?

Well, sort of.

Yogurts advertised as containing probiotics have to, as you now know, have strains in the billions. Most yogurts only have them in the millions. When you first hear that, it sounds like you are being bathed in strains, but the actual amount falls way short of what would be effective. And the journey through your intestines and its stomach acids will leave very few of those strains intact. It's why probiotic supplements delivery systems are via enteric-coated capsules. Enteric-coated capsules protect probiotics until they get to the intestines, where the capsules are digested and the probiotics are released.

But we'll keep believing the hype. We'll eat Go-Gurt, which was actually invented by a Brigham Young Professor, so in addition to being able to skateboard while downing this treat, we can also simultaneously get a subscription to *Watchtower*. By 1992, the yogurt industry was raking in over $1.135 billion.

Oh, by the way, in 1998, Dannon actually admitted that no Georgian over the age of 100 actually ate yogurt. And during the 2014 Sochi Olympics, Russia actually prevented the US from receiving a massive shipment of Chobani. I guess they thought they were legal PEDs and thus would pass muster in Doping Control. Of course, we all know who the real dopes are.

When you pack in over 400,000 at the most famous music festival ever, held in upstate New York in 1969, you are going to have some logistical problems. In addition to the massive amounts of people clogging up the roads leading to Woodstock, and the nightmare of going to the bathroom under normal conditions—much less under the influence of all sorts of illegal substances, including the Brown Acid—you might not be so quick in adding "food" to a list as long as the wait between acts. But it was a thing. A serious one. Nathan's Hot

Dogs backed out when the venue location was changed, and the hired company of Food for Love was ill-prepared for the mass of flesh, so showing their anti-Woodstock movement by going with their baser, capitalist instincts, they began charging outrageous prices, such as $1 for a hot dog instead of their usual quarter. Hell, even Dixie cups of water poured from local garden hoses fetched $1 per cup. Some food trucks assembled at the bottom of the hill, but leaving your tent or blanket or wherever your space happened to be entailed walking miles to get supplies, and thus forfeiting your space where you might actually hear (much less see) Jimi Hendrix mutilate the Star-Spangled Banner.

But the Woodstock promoters had also brought in Hugh Romney, better known as Wavy Gravy, and his famous commune, known as the Hog Farm Collective. He was also a card-carrying member of Ken Kesey's Merry Pranksters. And on Sunday morning, from the stage, Wavy Gravy announced "Breakfast in Bed for 400,000." And for many, that "breakfast in bed" was a cup of granola. The Hippies, and a group of people better known for partying with Hell's Angels and tripping them out on their first acid trip (and making their East Coast counterpart, Timothy Leary, look like a choir boy—except for the fact that he was the one name-checked in that Moody Blues song), were actually responsible for not only preventing a lot of festival-goers from starving, but also for spreading the knowledge, love, and need for cardboard and wood chippings as food.

Granola actually started out as granula, a concoction made out of oatmeal, wheat flour, and cornmeal by Dr. John Harvey Kellogg— yeah, *that* Kellogg. But a certain Dr. James Caleb Jackson actually created it first, sued Kellogg, and thus the name was altered to granola.

After Woodstock spread the food East, Heartland Natural Cereal mass-marketed the first granola, which came out in 1972. Vermont became such ground zero for it, which explained how it soon became known as the Crunchy Granola State. Many of the original hippies came to rest there, which is how we got Ben & Jerry's that gave us ice cream flavors such as Wavy Gravy, Cherry Garcia, and Phish Food.

So granola soon became co-opted by Big Cereal such as Quaker, Kellogg's and General Mills. And true to form, they corrupted the original recipe by adding fructose, corn syrup, and the myriad of ways one can say "sugar," thus making granola a not-so-healthy snack completely in opposition to how it was originally intended. But the government blew that one by actually doing something right, and the 1990 Nutrition Labeling and Education Act meant manufacturers were required to print detailed nutrition labels on their wares so we could actually see what kind of swill they were feeding us, starting in May of 1994.

Back in the 60s, TV ran PSAs for what a good breakfast was considered: eggs, bacon, buttered toast, coffee, and orange juice. In an act of surprising conscience, they left out the after-breakfast cigarette. They were obviously in league with the American College of Cardiology with their obvious efforts to drum up business. More than half a century later, we are encouraged to eat probiotic yogurt, granola with all kinds of sweeteners, tap water bottled by Nestlé, and orange juice, as The Florida Orange and Citrus Growers were quite the powerful lobby. Just ask your local politician.

So we blew it, as we always have, by being the obedient servants of mass advertising campaigns and the agencies that mine every algorithm they can about us so they know exactly how to get into our wallets and bloodstreams. Perhaps we should all look forward to the day we are all microchipped, and information, including advertising, is directly uploaded into our cerebral cortex—as so wonderfully portrayed by Harvey Keitel in *Saturn 3*. At least we could still play outside while we serve our corporate masters.

CONAN O'BRIEN

So we don't have Conan O'Brien on TV anymore. Not really. Oh sure, he'll do the occasional special and we'll see him on Instagram from time to time, but not where he should be: hosting late night TV. We had him, dammit. He was perfect, first taking over for Letterman and being groomed to be the true successor to Johnny Carson, but he ended up taking it on the chin from Leno and now we have Jimmy Fallon. And that really blows. Carson was great because he seemed like a volcano, always ready to erupt. It might be his ignoring the first national appearance of a stand-up comedian by not inviting him over to a sit-down, or his possibly flinging an envelope right into Ed McMahon's eye (no wonder he drank) while playing *Karnak the Magnificent*. And you knew that there would always be the chance of absolutely filthy double entendres being exchanged with the ingenue du jour. O'Brien gave us the Masturbating Bear and Triumph the Insult Comic Dog. Carson had Karnak, Aunt Blabby, and The Mighty Carson Art Players. Now try and think of one memorable character or interview Leno ever had. Exactly. So how did this happen? Where does the Fickle Finger of Blewdom land this time?

So, should a gangly, pasty-faced, red-haired, comic writer have the type of career deserving of making this list? His career underscores the entire concept of blewdom, but not by anything he did or didn't do, but by the asshats at television networks—and, to some degree, by us, the drones whose television-watching habits determine who gets on and stays on the tube.

His first noticeable gig was as a writer and sometimes background performer for *Saturday Night Live*. Two of his more well-known recurring skits were Mr. Short-Term Memory and The Girl Watchers, which always starred Tom Hanks and Jon Lovitz as two losers who couldn't pick up a hooker on the Vegas Strip back in the 70s.

His next stop was as a writer for *The Simpsons*, where his surreal comedy chops helped turn the show away from its more traditional sitcom format. With episodes such as "Marge vs the Monorail," "Homer Goes to College," and "Treehouse of Horror IV," the sitcoms soon morphed into a mashup of The Bundys meets Salvador Dali. But it was his one-time friend with benefits, Lisa Kudrow, who first suggested that he come out from behind his typewriter—or computer or intern transcribing slave—and start performing. He was reluctant. After all, writers aren't in front of the camera. Well, tell that to Mel Brooks, Woody Allen, and Steve Martin. And Lorne Michaels agreed, so when David Letterman stepped down from *Late Night,* Conan was tapped to become his replacement, sending him into a brief coma, face down in the *Simpsons* writers' room shag carpet when given the news in 1993.

Writers are a known neurotic lot, so when going in front of the camera, the pasty-white, red-haired, pompadour boy was nervous, fidgety, and often displayed his Harvard education, producing accusations of being the worst type of vermin to Middle America: an East Coast elite. The early ratings and reviews didn't bode well for a long and successful career behind the desk. Cancellation was whispered constantly among the NBC suits. But Conan seemed to be an acquired taste, and slowly, the show gained momentum among young, male viewers, and websites started to pop up dedicated to the show and its unlikely host.

He was going viral before anyone knew to call it that. He helmed the show for fifteen years.

Conan got the call-up that he was going to The Show, which meant hosting *The Tonight Show*. But lackluster ratings meant that the Suits at NBC were getting nervous. How soon they forgot that their stalwart shows, *Cheers* and *Seinfeld,* underwhelmed in their first seasons, but were kept around out of faith and the fact that rarely are there a bunch of potential hit shows in the pipeline, waiting to usurp the failing show blocking their ascent. But network Heads of Programming and Development have and remain the poster children for blewdom, as they were the ones that greenlit shows such as *My Mother the Car, Manimal,* and *Cop Rock.* A little scheme was hatched to move Leno's show out of its primetime slot to *The Tonight Show's* slot of 11:35 p.m., and to bump *The Tonight Show* to 12:05 a.m., technically making it The Fucking Way Too Early Show. Conan told the Suits to pound sand, so with a small transfer of $45 million to Conan's bank account, Leno was returned to his previous hosting duties and NBC blew the pooch—which, for some reason, sounds less nasty than "screwed."

Conan did what a creative person who signed a legal contract would do: he took his show on the road, and in 2010, embarked on his The Legally Prohibited from Being Funny on Television Tour. When the legal restrictions were lifted, Conan found himself back with hosting duties for the TBS show *Conan,* which ran from 2010–2021.

In 2015, he again took his live show on the road and made stops in such unlikely places as Cuba, Armenia, and South Korea. He even dipped his toe into North Korea, proving just how "Gangnam Style" his comedy was.

So The End wasn't actually near; it had damn well arrived. Conan did it "His Way," did it well and then got the "Exit Stage Left" for his efforts. He'll pop up from time to time on awards shows and who knows where, but we're stuck with Fallon, Kimmel, and a not-quite-as-funny Steven Colbert as he was on *The Colbert Report.* So the dimbulbs at NBC blew it, which was hardly news. They make news when they hit, not when they miss, and we also blew it...again. We had our chance at a Conan *Tonight Show* for decades, and we didn't tune in because of ...what? We were missing Leno?

And speaking of comedy, we really couldn't handle having two comedy networks on cable? We did once: Ha! and The Comedy Channel both launched at roughly the same time. The Comedy Channel premiered in 1989 and Ha! In 1990. They were very different in format and programming. The Comedy Channel had unconventional programs, weird talk shows, and hosts introducing clips from standup routines in addition to showing classic comedies from the 70s and 80s—such as *Young Frankenstein* and *Kentucky Fried Movie*. They also had reruns of *Monty Python's Flying Circus*. Ha! featured classic comedies from the 50s through the 70s such as *The Steve Allen Show* (better than Leno!), Groucho Marx's *You Bet Your Life, The Jack Benny Show, Candid Camera,* and *The Phil Silvers Show.*

But the channels couldn't even break into the New York market and neither had more than ten million subscribers, so the two behemoth parent companies, HBO and Viacom, decided to merge them in 1990 to create Comedy Central. Now as grateful as we should be for Jon Stewart and *The Daily Show*, couldn't we actually have had both of the original networks? We have way more than needed news, sports, and food networks, but God forbid we have more than one channel to try and get a chuckle. Of course, we were also unable to keep The Puppy Channel, although Animal Planet comes close. MeTV is great for watching endless reruns of *Gilligan's Island, The Beverly Hillbillies,* and *Carol Burnett.* So guess we're stuck with Vice's *Dark Side of the Ring* for alternative laughs to Comedy Central.

We blew it...yet again.

BURWELL VS HOBBY LOBBY

I would not like them
here or there
I would not like them
Anywhere
I don't believe in birth control
I'll strike it down
You little troll

Thus reads one of the stanzas in the Hobby Lobby employee hand-book called *Teen Eggs and Sperm*, written by its owner, Billionaire Evangelical Christian, David Green, who goes by the pen name Dr. Suess. Because when you own a giant arts and crafts chain, you obviously believe that your employees must be fornicating like demented weasels. Plus, the thinking was the more offspring the employees produced, the greater the pipeline would be for future employees, thus sidestepping the annoying process of advertising for help, interviewing, hiring, and training. Hobby Lobby could be to Evangelical Christians as the jewelry trade is to Hasidic Jews.

This was not always the thought process. Even Justice Scalia, as conservative a justice that has ever served on the Supreme Court, once believed that if you use religious beliefs as a reason to defy neutral laws, you would "make the professed doctrines of religious belief superior to the law of the land, and in effect to permit every citizen to become a law unto himself." He did just as he believed. You seek precedence for making decisions in the present, and in citing the 1878 case, *Reynolds v. the United States*, he did exactly that. But in 2006, The Supreme Court upheld the Religious Freedom Restoration Act in *Gonzales v. O Centro Espirita* which was just another way of telling women that they were shit out of luck. Obviously, the Religious Right never consulted with an obstetrician/gynecologist to learn that there are actually eight uses for the pill other than preventing pregnancy, such as making endometriosis bearable or even helping to prevent some forms of cancer. But to the fire and brimstone owner of Hobby Lobby, not only should every sperm seek an egg but every sperm has the right to plant their flag in an egg, and anything that interferes with their God-given right to swim upstream like a salmon, should at least be given a hearty pat on the flagellum. And they would be Goddamned if their employee-provided health insurance would be forced to pay for that. In that particular case, there were no chants of "build the wall, and make Hobby Lobby pay for it."

So the case started in the lower courts in 2012, where the United States Court of Appeals at the 10th Circuit parroted the Mitt Romney rallying cry of "corporations are people," and they ruled that Hobby Lobby was a person who had religious freedom. It never occurred to them that if a person can obstruct pregnancy prevention, then perhaps they should be forced to pay child support. Having kids can be an expensive Hobby (Lobby); preventing them, not so much.

As the case wound its way through the courts, dozens of amicus briefs ("amicus" is just legalese for "friends of the court," or "third parties who would provide seemingly relevant information due to their special interests in order to influence the court"), including one filed by the American Freedom Law Center which claimed birth control would harm women because men would only want them for the "satisfaction of their own desires." That attempted to suggest that women would only agree to having sex if it had the ability of procreation. Anyone who thought that obviously never attended a frat party, or any party in college or high school, or drive-in dates. Or went to a bar. Or actually liked sex. Or knew what sex was. Another brief claimed that contraceptives led to the "maximization of sexual activity." Well...yeah. But considering the level of anger in this country now, imagine how quickly it would go to Defcon 1 if you prohibited sexual activity unless the purpose was to make another "you," with a probable outcome of it being uglier and dumber.

Oral arguments (oh, the irony) went longer than usual, and they all came down to one concept: that employers had the right to impose their religious beliefs on their employees, and with a court that had been growing more conservative, the ruling went Hobby Lobby's way.

The case, as most legal cases do, spiraled into the weird argument that for-profit corporations were people and people have religious beliefs and you can't force them to pay for things that go against that belief. The other side argued that corporations exist to make money, and thus having any say in their employees' rights when it came to third-party health insurance coverage was silly, which then created the counter argument that, sure, corporations were in it for the filthy lucre, but they often used that filthy lucre for charitable causes that helped humanity, so female employees should just shut up and squeeze an aspirin between their legs, because contraceptives were verboten from

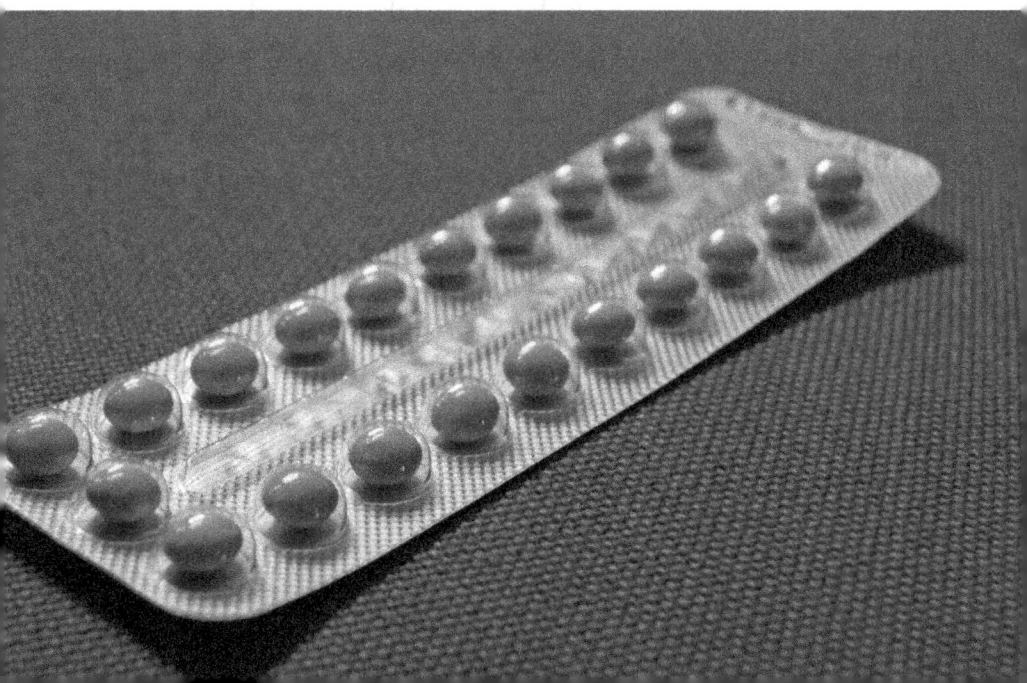

being covered by Hobby Lobby insurance plans. Another counter argument went that some religious beliefs were against paying taxes, so should they be exempt? This was followed by, um, no, because there was no remedy for not paying taxes, so double dumbass on you.

The Notorious RGB wrote the primary dissent:

"In a decision of startling breadth, the Court holds that commercial enterprises, including corporations, along with partnerships and sole proprietorships, can opt out of any law (saving only tax laws) they judge incompatible with their sincerely held religious beliefs. ... Compelling governmental interests in uniform compliance with the law, and disadvantages that religion-based opt-outs impose on others, hold no sway, the Court decides, at least when there is a 'less restrictive alternative.' And such an alternative, the Court suggests, there always will be whenever, in lieu of tolling an enterprise claiming a religion-based exemption, the government, i.e., the general public, can pick up the tab. The Court, I fear, has ventured into a minefield."

Mic drop!!!!

The Supreme Court told Hobby Lobby's female employees, who obviously weren't driving Porsches or Mercedes into work, that they should only do the nasty if they wanted kids or suck it up, buttercup (pun intended), and pay for your eighteen-year responsibility out of your own damn pocket. It also affirmed the slippery slope opinion that scientific and medical opinions could be ignored if certain people and businesses found them icky. But hey, what could go wrong with that? It's not like anyone was trying to overturn *Roe v. Wade*...right?

The Blew Factor on this one was off the charts. You start with The Supreme Court, and then work your way down to the Presidents who nominated the justices that voted in favor of Hobby Lobby, then to the Senators who confirmed them, and then to us, the voters, who voted in the Senators and then to the lobbyists, corporations, and superpacs that funded the Senators so they could influence us wishy-washy voters. The entire mess can often seem like a chicken or egg question, as long as nobody can prevent the egg from hatching another chicken.

HASHTAG

Led Zeppelin's Communication Breakdown was released in our magic year of 1969, and maybe they weren't predicting social media, but they could have been. Twitter, The Avis Rent-A-Car of social media, premiered the hashtag on August 23, 2007. Some yutz named Chris Messina copied it from a social media company called Jaiku, which was a Finnish version of Twitter that actually came out a month before Twitter did. Messina was the perfect inventor of such a gizmo, as his Wikipedia entry (perfect!) describes him as a "blogger, product consultant, technology evangelist and speaker"—in other words, in todayspeak, "a ne'er do well who got paid truckloads of money for doing things that have no actual value except to create a monetary mirage, similar to Bitcoin." The verbiage associated with the hashtag was mind boggling, #fuckmenow. A smattering of such words and expressions are: metadata tag, folksonomy, taxonomy, markup language, eavesdropper, wormhole, contextualization, and of course, hyperlinks.

Messina, not to be confused with Loggins, wanted to make sure that people, or "users," could understand everything they saw on their timeline, because before the hashtag, Twitter was indecipherable with only 140 characters allowed—now upped to 280—so sure, anything to organize that chaos would be much appreciated. Messina actually found some initial hesitancy (horrors!) to the use of the hashtag, as critics claimed that it made a simple platform "cumbersome." Those people obviously never had to untangle a 30-foot, coiled, princess phone cord to understand what the word "cumbersome" involving a communication device actually meant.

The 2007 San Diego Fires became ground zero for the popularity of hashtags. Twitter users could instantly find conversations and threads discussing the story, as reading the newspaper or turning on any of a dozen news channels was simply too much work. Seeing a good thing, Twitter began to hyperlink all hashtags in tweets to Twitter search results for the hashtagged word, which soon introduced trending topics—but the good news was that Twitter created an algorithm to block attempts to spam trending lists, which is why "fetch" never happened. Well, maybe now that there is a Hashtags.org site, we can all dedicate more time and energy trying to figure out the etiquette for using a symbol that once was only used to play tic tac toe or stand in for the word "number."

For the #OKBoomer people like me, the hashtag is just another level into the cacophony of blewdom. Tech people kept creating social media platforms for us to spend hours figuring out ways to communicate with each other without actually saying anything. We can create names and watch them trend, just as Australians do at their rugby matches when, an incomparable number of times, some hooligan in the crowd will yell *Aussie! Aussie!* just to hear the response of *Oi! Oi! Oi!* validate their existence, at least temporarily. Eventually, the stadium full of drunk Aussies are bored of the continued attempts at the chant and will pound the next offender until he feels like a shrimp that spent a little too much time on the barby.

The techies create something weird and we follow like lemmings to make that something into a much bigger something, until our entire lives are spent sorting out the bigger and bigger somethings to kill our lives with so we don't actually do or accomplish anything. So once again, the people who blew it the most are us, the Great Unwashed, who continue to figure out ways to stay on our laptops and phones rather than be. But to the guy that created this epic timewaster, I say, #YouSuckMessina.

SOUTHERN ROCK BANDS

At one time, our radio airwaves and concert venues were chock full of southern rock band music. During the late 60s and throughout the 80s, we were treated to the twin guitar attack, slide guitar virtuosos, twangy R&B covers, soaring, melodic harmonies, and just songs that revitalized the idea of Dixie. Bands like Marshall Tucker, The Outlaws, Little Feat, The Allman Brothers Band, Wet Willie, The Atlanta Rhythm Section, The Amazing Rhythm Aces, Dr. John, ZZ Top, 38 Special, Molly Hatchet, Lynyrd Skynyrd, Elvin Bishop, The Band, Blackfoot, Black Oak Arkansas, The Ozark Mountain Daredevils, The Georgia Satellites, Pure Prairie League, David Allan Coe, and The Fabulous Thunderbirds could even make a Boston Brahmin go out and buy a pair of Tony Lama boots to kick up the dust at a local hoedown. They were "Rambling Men" who "Drove Old Dixie Down" as the "Midnight Rider" searched for his "Dixie Chicken," and "Jim Dandy" just had to "Keep On Smilin'" as "The Wild-Eyed Southern Boys" made you sure you "Kept Your Hands to Yourself" while singing your aching ballad to "Amy," because dang it, she sure was a "Free Bird." You may start swaying your Bic lighter in the air now—or use it to torch the book for that last, hideous, run-on sentence.

The music drew on its roots of country, blues, and even bluegrass from the 50s and emphasized boogie rhythms, scorching-fast lead guitars, and the values, aspirations, excesses, and demons of the Southern working-class, blue-collar adults who would rather break conventions than attend one. They could incorporate the flute, as The Marshall Tucker Band did with "Heard It In a Love Song" and "Can't You See" or Charlie Daniels's fiddle on his iconic "The South's Gonna Do It Again" and "The Devil Went Down to Georgia."

There was an offshoot of Southern Rock known as Country Rock, as the bands from that genre didn't necessarily have to have Southern roots. Many came from California, where Bakersfield was a hotbed of the California country song. Bands and artists such as Poco, The Flying Burrito Brothers, The Nitty Gritty Dirt Band, Emmylou Harris, Linda Ronstadt, and even The Eagles grew out of the folk music sounds of Bob Dylan, which directly mothered The Band, The Byrds, and Buffalo Springfield, with their Canadian singer/writer/guitarist, Neil Young.

So what happened? Did the genre die in the flaming wreckage of Lynyrd Skynyrd's doomed flight? Oh sure, there are still a smattering of artists that can be grouped in the Country or Southern Rock milieu. As much maligned as the 70s are when people think of music, it was a very fertile time. Virtually every type of musical genre found at least a temporary sweet spot on the radio, in the charts, and in venues for live music.

The gamut included corporate rock, garage rock, indie rock, prog rock, punk rock, new wave, disco, reggae, and of course, Southern and country rock. Movie soundtracks also featured and helped to boost the popularity of all of these genres, with *Urban Cowboy, Saturday Night Fever, The Harder They Come* and *Blank Generation* showing how a film and its accompanying soundtrack could boost a musical style into the stratosphere. But one of the biggest supporters of Southern/Country Rock was Capricorn Records. It grew out of the Walden Brothers, who managed and represented R&B recording artists such as Otis Redding, Sam & Dave, Al Green, and Percy Sledge. After forming Capricorn Records in 1969, The Walden Bros then got a distribution deal with Atlantic Records and built a recording studio in Macon, Georgia. The design of the recording studio differed from most others, and Capricorn also employed a group of musicians who would not only back many of the artists who recorded there but would also engineer and produce some of the most famous Southern Rock albums of all time.

Alan Walden heard and loved the slide guitar playing on Wilson Pickett's cover of "Hey Jude," and he tracked Duane Allman down to sign him, which then helped create The Allman Brothers Band. In 1971, The Allman Brothers Band would release *At Fillmore East,* which went gold, Capricorn's first. This jumpstarted the entire musical brand, which allowed for more diversity than the moniker would seem to permit, as it blended country, jazz, blues, and rock.

Between the years of 1969 and 1979, Capricorn produced nine platinum albums, 17 gold albums, and five gold singles.

But The Allman Brothers split up in 1976 (although they would reform multiple times), and the 70s recession hit Capricorn records hard, and the huge debt load they carried caused their distributor at the time, PolyGram Records, to file a lawsuit seeking all collateral and assets to repay the loan they made to the label in 1977. The rats began

deserting the sinking ship, and many of Capricorn's artists fled the label. The Allman Brothers sued to prevent their greatest hits album from being issued.

Capricorn reappeared in Nashville in the 90s and had some success, but it wasn't the same. In the 70s, the label helped foment Macon Georgia as a vibrant music scene and helped the Country/Southern Rock genre flourish. So it's tricky as to where the blew factor should be assigned. There are still remnants of the Country/Southern Rock sound today, but it nowhere near resembling the heyday of the 70s. The lawsuits chasing the label out of its flush position and Lynyrd Skynyrd's plane crash both happened in 1977. So should the fingers point at the people in charge of Capricorn Records' finances and the fueler for Lynyrd Skynyrd's Conair CV-240? Or were the problems less or more complicated than that? Perhaps the aforementioned film *Urban Cowboy* had a little something to do with it. The film made the desire to ride a mechanical bull, dance country line and country swing in order to impress all the phony cowgirls, and suck down bottle after bottle of Lone Star Beer a trend, and trends, be they in music, fashion, dance, or slang, never last. The 80s was a decade made for the quick rise and fall of trends, and music, fashion, and certain drinks and drugs were all a part of the tendencies that rose the harsh sine wave of fast-rising/ hard-falling rages.

A lot of the music that became hugely popular in the 70s, while obviously still hanging around, just isn't in the zeitgeist to the level it was then. Perhaps it's just a state of affairs that nobody as good as a Marshall Tucker Band and The Outlaws in Southern Rock; Bob Marley, Toots Maytall, and Jimmy Cliff in Reggae; and The Bee Gees in disco have emerged over the decades. The whimsey of consumer tastes points to the possibility that at some undetermined point a new star could rise, reigniting the flames of Southern/Country Rock, again. There has never been another Picasso, Dali, Hemingway, or Fitzgerald in the arts. The Collective Unconscious often predicted that everything old would be new again. Lobster-bib-sized ties and leisure suits have thankfully not returned, There are no doo-wop groups charting, but their influence can still be heard. The biggest hurdle toward seeing a genuine revival of the classic Southern and Country rock sound has been the homogenization of the song stylings. Perhaps artists are following Cary Grant's credo of choosing a style in the middle of fashion. So Taylor Swift could be considered a country artist when she's clearly a pop artist with some country influences peeping out. The question in order to really lay the *who blew it* scenario is this: have Southern/Country artists watered down their sound in order to reach a wider audience, or have we, the audience, become less tolerant of certain musical styles, causing fewer artists to practice them?

TELEPHONE LINE

Film, television and song writers understood early on what a powerful yet frightening device the telephone was. Rod Sterling terrified an old woman who began receiving calls from her former fiancé that she ignorantly killed in a car crash. Billy Mumy talked to his dead grandmother who urged him to kill himself on a toy telephone so that he could join her. The iconic babysitter and the man upstairs from many a horror film, such as *When A Stranger Calls* (1979), where the police eventually trace the threatening calls to inside the house and plead with her to "Get out now!" The horror trope was wonderfully parodied in the first *Scream* film, and was based on an actual incident from 1950. Part of Spencer Tracy's incredible speech at the end of *Inherit the Wind* included the line: "You can have a telephon,e but you lose privacy and the charm of distance." ELO's song mourned over a lost relationship because the couple simply didn't communicate, and if only she picked up the phone, then he wouldn't have to live in twilight. Deborah Harry was left hanging on the telephone because once again, some rat bastard just didn't want to pick it up and listen to whatever screechy ad hominems she wanted to toss his way.

A lot of this longing for someone to pick up was supposed to have been fixed in 1971 when Casio developed the first commercially viable answering machine. Now, not being home or refusing to pick up (which really wasn't a thing then), had been usurped by a simple machine that recorded the desperate pleas of the person trying to reach you. Without caller ID, we had no idea who it was, including if it was a killer, so we had to pick up. And we did. But the answering machine also introduced several more levels of stress that even Spencer Tracy hadn't thought of. First was the leaving of the outgoing message. Nothing captured this existential crisis more than the 2003, seven-minute film *This is John* from the Duplass Brothers, Mark and Jay, who became stalwarts of the Mumblecore film movement (editor's note: I stupidly rejected this film for my 2003 film festival because, well, I was a dumbass). The film had John recording, rerecording, and rererecording his outgoing phone message until he ended up in a quivering, bumbling puddle of a person, breaking down so completely as he recognized that would be judged and identified completely by his brief greeting. On the other end of the spectrum was *Seinfeld's* George Costanza's phone message, sung to the theme song from the TV show, *The Greatest American Hero*, where he giddily screened his calls while he warbled to callers that "Believe it or not, he's not home." And that became the biggest downside to the answering machine - the ability to screen calls when you *were* home. The device morphed from something that would allay your fears of what you were missing while doing errands or in the shower or having sex with hopefully somebody, to the supposition of technological communication: my non-response *is* my response. That bit of folderol far outstripped the other annoyances, such as obscene messages or pranks left by friends, family, enemies, or psychopathic shut-ins with nothing better to do than the random rants left on an anonymous person's answering machine. Because that's the zero-sum game of most communication today.

In 1995, *Match* created the first online dating site and thus, all the inconveniences of meeting people in person so that they can instantly see what you look like, sound like, and act like in public could be totally eliminated by creating a profile of who you wished to be in the hopes that your bait will now actually attract rather than repel the person you are imagining a hook-up with. But that wasn't the most insidious aspect of the concept, not even close. We were always able to

lie in person about who we were, what we did, and what we were interested in. We just couldn't fake the looks, but that wasn't as much of a
liability as we thought. If someone wasn't interested, you would know
it right away either by their refusal to talk with you, or by their dumping out of the conversation with the lamest excuse, but regardless of
your hurt feelings, at least you knew right then and there and you were
free to pursue your life—miserably, but unburdened by false hopes.
Now we're required to send incredibly clever and pithy notes to the
person of whom we have interest and then hope we receive a response
that validates our brilliance. And that's what the answering machine's
biggest downside taught us: that if you ignore them, maybe they'll go
away. No more, "I have to wash my hair," or "my dad needs me to do
something that day." You're just ignored. Nada, zip, bupkis. At least an
in-person rejection had a communication element to it, and you could
always find a physical flaw in the other person to help you rationalize
your rejection, allowing you to convince yourself that you were the one
who dodged a bullet. But now you're just left hanging. Before answering machines, you could at least delude yourself into believing the
other party was either in the hospital, dead, or possibly trapped under
something heavy as Billy Crystal opined in *When Harry Met Sally.*
Stripping away our delusional and rationalizing behaviors is simply
horrible for our fragile psyches. You lost the ability to concoct reasons
for your rejection that had nothing to do with the fact that you had a
goiter the size of a football, the halitosis of an elderly chihuahua, or
the conversational skills of *Rain Man.* The answering machine should
have prepared us for this day when we came back home after being out
all day and did not seeing the blinking light, indicating no messages, or
worse: heard the robotic voice basically tell us that we were unloved,
unworthy of love, and that we will die alone and be eaten by our 25
cats.

1994 delivered the first online job-search website in Monster. 1995
gave us CareerBuilder, 1996 brought us Hot Jobs, and 2003, LinkedIn. Just like Match, or EHarmony and JDate, we could put our profile out there, pursue a plethora of job openings, and attempt to land

that next great step in our career without getting our fingers dirty from newspaper ink. And as they always did, algorithms could be our Waterloo. They look at keywords and ignore things like training, years at a certain type of job, or skill, so that the kid right out of college will be equal to someone with 20 years in the field. Many sites are aggregators, culling data from other sites and giving you listings that were filled weeks, if not, months ago. And similar to that potential dream date you viewed on Match, chances were you didn't hear a peep from the potential employer, thus employing the soul-crushing, "my non-response *is* my response" yet again. And it got worse. Some companies send you a link to take an assessment, which is timed. You receive a bunch of questions not unlike the ones you had to frustratingly answer in high school: "Al is traveling southwest on a bus traveling 35 mph with a 10 mph headwind with stops every 15 minutes. Susan is preparing lunch for her in-laws and her neighbors, as she lost a bet with her boss. What time will Mike serve Debbie her divorce papers, if it's Tuesday and raining?" And that assessment can appear on a job application for a pizza delivery gig that you didn't really want, but now you have to feel bad about yourself before they ignore you.

This practice of shrugging off our communication applies to every device. Text messages, emails, and every way we communicate with each other has an element of intentionally disregarding the other party to exert our power, leverage, and control. Gone are the days when we were just putting our key into the lock of our front door when we heard the phone ring and practically broke the door down because buying a new door was perceived as less of a hassle than actually missing a phone call. The same goes for the dreaded call while in the shower. Risking a broken leg, or an embarrassing concussion when slipping and bashing our head against the toilet is nothing compared to not knowing who just called or when they might call again. It could have been the person we left the creepy note on their windshield, begging them to call us, or the employer, about to offer us a six-figure salary to save their company from folding. We used to value our communication. As a child, when you made the tin can connected with a string communication system, you didn't refuse to answer just because your friend was around the corner of your house and you couldn't see each other. That was the point—you could still talk to each other even when an obstacle came between you. Now we are the obstacle. We struggle to find love, careers, or the time to even see each other, as we're too busy using ways to show other people how "too busy" we are to respond. We created a world in which there are more ways than ever to communicate and find the things that make us whole, but instead, we chose to use them as psychological weapons. Our collective self-esteem has been lowered to the point that we're all just frayed insulation on a fiber optic wire. We literally have the world in our palms, and we blew it.

POP GOES THE CULTURE

New York, Pairs, London, Vulture
Everybody talk about...pop culture
Talk about...pop culture

OK, those weren't the lyrics to M's 1979, one-hit wonder "Pop Muzik"...but they could have been.

The term "popular culture" was coined in the mid-19th century, and it referred to the cultural traditions of the people, in contrast to the "official culture" of the state or governing classes.

Its modern interpretation unofficially began during the 1950s with rock n' roll, TV, Dick Clark, the hula hoop, and transistor radios, and continues today with every new form of mass communication that allows elements from certain peoples, cultures, and geographic settings to be adopted by others not originally in their tribes. The term "pop culture" became mainstream during the 1980s, so it fits the paradigm of post-1969 contributions to the current state of blewdom.

What is considered "pop culture" today? In simple terms, pop culture can be defined as a blend of ideas, images, attitudes, and perspectives that characterize a given culture and are adored by the mainstream population. Modern pop culture commenced with the baby boomers, who influenced the pop culture revolution through their disposable income.

Ah, so the expression, "OK, Boomer." A generation who are *not* Baby Boomers actually coined a phrase about them which has, in turn, become part of the lexicon of modern pop culture. Irony: another classic sign of pop culture.

Traditionally, popular culture was associated with poor education and with the lower classes, as opposed to the "official culture" and higher education of the upper classes.

Examples of popular culture come from a wide array of genres, including popular music, print, cyber culture, sports, entertainment, leisure, fads, advertising, and television. Some sporting events, such as the World Cup and the Olympics, are consumed by a world community.

And in all of these things, pop culture in entertainment and sports have contributed mightily to the US's massive problem of low self-esteem. Pop culture has helped create a ubiquitous Potemkin village which has impacted every facet of our society and could be seen as the Unifying Theory behind the vast majority of these essays defining the reasons how and why, collectively, we all blew it. We actually elected a person for the highest office whose bluster, self-aggrandizement, and vile spewing against all who don't share his facade has released and intensified the massive infection that had been growing inside and among us for decades. His bloviations did nothing to conceal his well-earned, cripplingly low self-esteem and his facility for gaslighting his base, but more to convince himself that his prima facie of the world

was correct. All this underscored the current decade's problem with looking at others only as they reflected the horror of when we stared into the mirror ourselves. We would rather blow up Democracy than live with the primal urges that bubbled out of us to the point where we ignored and, in some cases, welcomed disease rather than being a truly populist nation and take one for the team so the team could repay in kind. And stay alive. Death, while permeating every culture and tripe in history, has never exactly been popular—at least when it comes to our own. Now, allowing and even fomenting death in others has always been extremely popular.

We began our excursion in 1969 where Captain America and Billy proved to us that being "Born to Be Wild" was the ultimate adventure, only to have that philosophy crash down hard with the utterance of "We Blew It," followed by the literal blowing us all physically up and metaphorically away. We thought we reached the mountaintop with the Peace, Love, Sex, and Granola stylings of Woodstock and the Moon Landing, only to come back down to Earth with Hate, Violence, Hell's Angels, "Sympathy for the Devil" murder at Altamont, and the major malfunction of Challenger. We marveled at the chase scene climaxing in the Good Guy catching and killing the Bad Guy in *The French Connection* in 1971 only to see it inevitably end in a fiery explosion into concrete barriers with *Vanishing Point* just a few months later. The messages weren't so much mixed as they were competing, and the wrong ones seemed to win.

We stared into the abyss of The Idiot Box and we found the false promises of the Modern Nuclear Family of *The Brady Bunch,* and while we may have lusted after whoever struck our fancy, we never really felt they had anything real to offer. *All in the Family* gave us nothing but realism, but did we feel better if we identified with the Bigot with a Heart of Gold, a wife whose decency was promulgated through her dingbattery, a hippie whose nome de plume of Meathead was actually his true identifying characteristic, or a nasally, whiny but cute, Blonde Little Girl whose short skirts were matched by her attention span? But those families seemed positively altruistic compared to The Bundys of

Married with Children, realistic compared to The Huxtables of *The Cosby Show,* and those were supplanted by the surrealism of *Twin Peaks* and the fatalism of *My So-Called Life.* And when professional wrestling convinced us that the Heel was much more interesting than the Babyface, we actually cheered when The Danger invaded our living rooms. Yes, we were on the side of a crystal meth dealer, which might just be the all-time symbolic gesture that describes just where we're at. Film made us an offer we couldn't refuse, and TV gave it to us for six years—more, if you count the prequel.

Pop culture seemed to have been mocking us for decades in the Sunday funnies. *Peanuts* was on top in 1969, and Charlie Brown's catchphrase of "Good Grief" exhibited the yin and yang for the end of that tumultuous decade by putting almost an antonym together for us to chew on. A place where a maladjusted child opens a psychiatry booth while a dog fancies himself a World War I Flying Ace and has a real eye for art collection tries to distract from the fact that the *hero* is a bald loser who pines for friends, baseball success, and the unreachable, Little Red-Haired Girl.

Doonesbury defined the 80s with political satire and so many hot-button topics that many newspapers refused to run it—or only did so in their editorial section. Trudeau wasn't so much lampooning 80s culture, both pop and political, as he was skewering our undeniable debauchery—which didn't work out so well for the characters in the strip, or us.

Borrowing heavily from the drawing style of *Doonesbury,* the 90s *Bloom County* forwent showing us just how often and badly we were blowing it, and not only human characters, but an unnaturally hopeful and naive talking penguin, Opus, and the fetid, putrid, Bill the Cat, to let us know just how far down the drain we were circling. Computers often came alive and stalked us, but the strip soon became a parody of itself and morphed into *Outland,* which was basically the same strip with a different name, and we weren't buying it or even reading i—but there might not be any better representation of blowing it than the pithy yet expressive, *Ack* and *Thppt!*

Parents finally made an appearance in *Calvin and Hobbes*, and you can see how Calvin could go either way as an adult: he could either bow to the crushing of his soul due to his imagination being misunderstood by parents and teacher—resulting in his being dosed with Ritalin and sent to child psychologists until his predictable final breakdown—or, if his resistance to others doing all they could to blow it for him before he ever got started was stalwart, he might have represented the last, great hope we ever actually had within the pop-culture realm of comic strips. This is where creator Bill Watterson left us with his final strip, that had *Calvin and Hobbes* happily taking the sled out on a glorious, snowy day with the caveat, "Let's Go Exploring," being the last thing we read. Watterson never took a dime for merchandising or animated specials, and the main argument for blowing it with any reference to him is that there are no statues of him in any public square of schools, named either after him or his creations (and Calvin Coolidge doesn't count). Until that great wrong is rectified, consider it blown.

The 2000s brought us *Dilbert,* and what better representation of us did we have then an office drone and his co-workers plugging away in a futile effort to derive meaning from the life of the cubicle? *Dilbert* and the Mike Judge, 1999 film *Office Space* delivered the painful news of how the US already blew it to the extreme by developing and permitting this type of work life to exist. So the funny papers don't really exist anymore, as newspaper readership declines. Some migrated online, but that left the term "funny papers" to the ashcan of former times, which is where everything is going. As the Possum so perfectly declared in one of the best comic strips of all time, *Pogo,* "We have met the enemy and he is us."

There is no better metric of the extent of pop culture's influence than to see how it is portrayed in film. All of the music from *American Graffiti* was diegetic, exploding out of the various car radios, moving the narrative along until you actually arrived at the station and met Wolfman Jack. Radio was once fertile ground for filmmakers, as exhibited by *Play Misty For Me, FM, Radio Days, A Prairie Home Companion, Private Parts, Airheads,* and *American Hot Wax.* Every generation sub-Baby Boomer only knows DJs from hip hop and rap groups. Songs about DJs won't be played even on satellite radio stations, as their meaning will be lost, so say goodbye to songs such as "W.O.L.D." (Harry Chapin), "The Spirit of Radio" (Rush), "Politics of Dancing" (Re-flex), "Rapture" (Blondie), "Rapper's Delight" (Sugar Hill Gang), "Clap for the Wolfman" (The Guess Who), "Do You Remember Rock N Roll Radio?" (The Ramones), "Hey Mr. DJ" (Zhané), "DJ Culture" (Pet Shop Boys), and "I AM the DJ" (David Bowie). Video might have killed the radio star, but centralized programming and digital downloads killed the radio, the DJ, and everything that got us celebrating while cruising. The Buggles should consider reforming and recording an updated version, but the chorus wouldn't be as catchy.

The same goes for movies about record stores—or at least with great scenes that took place in them—another cultural artifact destroyed by *progress*. These films made us want to buy all the classics, and gave us an appreciation of vinyl. That beautiful scene of the needle being dropped on the records, and the character experiencing a song for the first time always got us. It was truly the best way to listen to music, and everything from the cover of the album to the inside liner notes gave us something to talk about. High Fidelity and Empire Records were the two films that actually centered around this once mighty icon that gave us all the feels for a cultural reference in its heyday. High Fidelity actually makes you yearn for the snarkiness of the record store snob, whose musical appreciation was so much better than yours and they never let you forget it, especially when your choices were presented at the cash register for payment and judgment. Empire Records featured the greatest plaid skirt ever, and it reminded us of the importance of fashion in pop culture—and even the fashion of the 90s can be missed, if given the right treatment. Try explaining to a Millennial or Generation Zer why Duckie, lip synching, and grinding against a wall of 80s records to Otis Redding's "Try a Little Tenderness" would make the girls weak in the knees. The guys used to practice it in their bedrooms so that one day, they could...well, make girls weak in the knees. Or guys, if that was their thing. That's what *Pretty in Pink* featured. If you were into French New Wave films, you loved *Vivre Sa Vie*. That movie actually wasn't about records. The theme was much darker than that, however, the French just know how to make a record store seem like a place for peace. The scene in the record store was so charming. That movie made you want to cut your bangs, smoke cigarettes, and listen to sad French music. *Before Sunrise* was 1995's must-see for its philosophical take on romance. So much sexual tension radiated from the scene where the two strangers were together in the listening booth. Something about the quality of sound and that moment where you find that sweet spot to listen to a tune no longer exists. *500 Days of Summer* put the Manic Pixie Dream Girl (Nathan Rabin's perfect description), Zooey Deschanel, in a record store to teach us how break-ups are done. Ringo Starr's "Stop" was used as a buffer to the awkward silence. It's wild how much a location can bring out the most intense debates over which Beatle is the best, and how digging through records with a lover really helped you to get to know them.

Getting nostalgic for nostalgia is akin to putting two mirrors facing each other. Every generation mourns the lost entities that form the images from their salad days, whose clarity grows fuzzier with each passing year. It's a natural occurrence, as we all equate youthful memories to lost innocence—until we really focus in and recall all the nonsense that occurred back then, and suddenly, things aren't looking so rosy. But progress is supposed to improve upon what we had, not always replace it—unless the replacement is so much cooler it makes us forget the former. If we were all riding around in flying cars as *The Jetsons* promised us, we wouldn't be so teary-eyed over the loss of giant fins, convertibles, or leaded, cheap gas. But the loss of grooving to tunes on our car radio or meeting friends at the local movie theater, even if it was a giant chain multiplex, removed another way to connect on a personal level with strangers simply due to the shared experience. But we mostly watch movies at home and buy our music online, and two strangers meeting in a parking lot in the middle of the night after another weekend bender, listening to the radio when suddenly the song starts skipping as the DJ went to take a leak, and you look over and see the stranger in the other car getting into the same skip just as you were, forced you just to get out of your car and introduce yourself to your fellow traveler—well, that's not happening ever again. Accepting the new shouldn't always mean destroying the old, because that blows it for everyone. Pop culture shouldn't mean actually popping it like a balloon.

BIG PHARMA

There are only two countries in the world that allow prescription drugs to advertise on television. The US is one. One thousand points if you can guess the other.

If you said New Zealand, congratulations. And I don't believe you.

The US consumer drug advertising boom on television began in 1997, when the FDA relaxed its guidelines relating to broadcast media. The Big Pharma lobbyists did their usual successful arm-twisting, combined with legal corruption and graft, to get the ruling they wanted. The results of the massive ad campaigns were predictable, as the compelling spots caused patients to petition their physicians and health-care providers to write out gaggles of scripts to alleviate mood disorders, cardiovascular and skin conditions, and other chronic ailments—and, of course, erectile dysfunction. The FDA is powerless to limit how much money the drug companies spend, or even to ban advertising for drugs with serious side effects. Such side effects are often read at the end of the ad by people whose primary occupation is to MC cattle auctions; their expertise at rapid and incoherent speech often has us missing the part where they say, "May cause anal bleeding, skin ruptures and death." And as any dyed-in-the-wool capitalist will tell you, increasing demand increases cost, so there is a causal relationship between the price of prescription drugs and the overall cost of health care to drugs' massive amounts of advertising.

One thing Madison Avenue has always excelled at is to terrify you of the dangers of *not* demanding pharmaceutical products. Any ad for drugs that are targeted for mood disorders and depression feature actors who are miserable and shows how their misery is making everyone around them despair—especially the children. But after popping a couple of pills, they are the most happy-go-lucky people, enjoying the little things in life and making everyone in their orbit just want to skip and whistle all day. The ads never suggest seeking therapy in addition to whatever chemical they want you to swallow twice a day. Just as drugs for diabetes don't illustrate how diet and exercise should be a part of the routine, mood disorder spots lie by omission. And erectile dysfunction cures show the beautiful wife just all smiles, implying their marital woes just disappeared once the boloney was operating at full capacity. But the agencies and drug manufacturers' consciences are clear due to the little caveat at the end of the side effects white noise, where the voice slows down to add, "Ask your doctor or pharmacist." But make sure the first has already taken out his script pad and scribbled the note to take to the second.

Drugs and their advertising bonanza aren't just an adult problem. American children lead the world in ADHD diagnoses by more than a two to one margin, at 11 percent compared to 5 percent for Brazil, China and Europe. Like PTSD—which morphed from "shell shock" to "battle fatigue" before landing on its current "PTSD" moniker— ADHD started out as "hyperkinetic impulse disorder." It wasn't until 1969 when the American Psychiatric Association (APA) recognized ADHD as a mental disorder. It was actually first mentioned in 1902, when a British pediatrician observed an abnormal defect of moral control in children who had normal intelligence. The FDA approved the drug Benzedrine as a medicine in 1936, and a pediatrician named Dr. Charles Bradley stumbled across its benefits to children whom he administered the drug to while seeking to study the loss of spinal fluid caused by severe headaches. Both nurses and teachers noticed an improvement in those children in both behavior and academic performance. The kids actually began calling the drug "arithmetic pills," which was somewhat chilling when you think about that potential marketing bonanza had the manufacturer or an ad agency got wind of it.

It took a while before the APA really acknowledged ADHD. In the first two editions of the *Diagnostic and Statistical Manual of Mental Disorders* (DSM), it was still referred to as "hyperkinetic impulse disorder," but in their 1980 edition, they changed the name of the disorder to "attention deficit disorder" (ADD), as it was easier to promote to the masses and convince them they needed drugs. Scientists believed hyperactivity was not a common symptom of the disorder, but they didn't poll mothers about their poor, vibrating children. This listing created two subtypes of ADD: ADD with hyperactivity and ADD without hyperactivity—kind of like Mounds and Almond Joy, only substituting "almonds" for "hyperactivity." The APA released a revised version of the DSM-III in 1987, in which they removed the hyperactivity distinction and changed the name to "attention deficit hyperactivity disorder" (ADHD), because it was a much cooler acronym. The APA combined the three symptoms (inattentiveness, impulsivity, and hyperactivity) into a single type and did not identify subtypes of the disorder, because who has the time to bother with subtypes? And with the name distinction becoming more known both in the medical community and among laymen, ADHD diagnoses began to soar, which, of course, was the point all along. They really kicked in with the No Child Left Behind Act of 2001. Now federal school funding was at stake. Tell a low-income community that some serious bucks could be forfeited unless the collective GPA spikes and you create a recipe where desperation becomes a pusher. Suddenly those school accountability laws led to a 59 percent increase in ADHD diagnoses in low-income areas. And with the diagnoses came treatment, and high on the list was the 1955 FDA approval of the psychostimulant known as Ritalin. Follow me for more drug recipes.

Novartis, the drug manufacturer of Ritalin, started advertising in magazines. Drug sales in the South boomed—which can't be connected to the fact that magazine subscriptions in the South were greater than other parts of the country...could it? So you have a perfect example of vertical marketing, or even a pyramid scheme. The APA determined the criteria for diagnosing mental health disorders in their sporadic publishing of the DSM. Doctors, health regulators, and Big Pharma relied on the DSM to base their diagnoses and recommend the proper treatments. The criteria for ADHD broadened in every subsequent DSM, and Big Pharma increased their advertising budgets to areas with failing students. Demand increased and supply followed. What's amazing is that we haven't (yet) seen the perfect storm of diagnosis and demand to produce a breakfast cereal called Ritalineos or Captain Adderall. Calvin might have been an entirely different kid if his mom bought one of those choices instead of Chocolate Frosted Sugar Bombs. Ritalin Boy Scouts evolved into Prozac Nation and the circle of life just kept on going. Millennials were the proving ground for ADHD, and they also lead in autism and asthma diagnoses. No wonder they came from helicopter parents. They needed the flailing arms just to achieve room temperature.

So the Blewdom factor here is off the charts. Between the APA, Big Pharma lobbyists, spineless weasel politicians that gladly took their shekels and passed laws without thinking about effect, the FDA, your family pediatrician, and even your own mom and dad don't get out of this unscathed. But at least they have an anthem, with Thomas Dolby's 1984 song, "Hyperactive."

THE HOODIE

The Hoodie actually started in the 1930s when Champion started sewing hoods on sweatshirts once it had developed methods for thicker materials—as who wants a thin hood over their head? They were used in mostly upstate New York to keep laborers warm during winter, as your typical company asshat was always grabbing your warm, woolen hat off your head and playing keep-away, so having your hat attached to your shirt made sense. But it didn't reach iconic status until 1976, when Rocky Balboa wore his gray hoodie running through the streets of Philadelphia. 1976 must have been a good year to have hoodies in running scenes in films, as *Marathon Man* featured Dustin Hoffman running wearing the same garment. Colleges and universities also began putting their names on hoodies so everyone could be cool to their school.

The 70s was also when hip hop culture exploded. American designer Norma Kamali incorporated the hoodie into her lines and put it on the catwalk, but the super skinny supermodels mistook them for a bathtub. One reporter termed them as "cool anonymity and menace," and what fashion-oriented thug could resist that? The 80s underlined the "menace" part, not so much the "cool," when FBI composite drawings of The Unabomber, Ted Kaczynski, depicted him wearing dark sunglasses and a hoodie. And with the ubiquitous pic of Kaczynski influencing a generation of ne'er-do-wells, it was inevitable

that the look would be incorporated into the guise of graffiti artists, skateboarders, punk rockers, and anyone else who wished to advertise their street cred and fly their freak flag to the mainstream.

The hoodie was supposed to be utilitarian, with it being designed as resort wear for grandmothers, and even Trendy Tummy Maternity offered one with concealed openings for breastfeeding (try not to think of that image now). But thanks to Ted, the hoodie's rep was tainted as something only for the seedy. Technically, it should have been seen as just the opposite. The hoodie eliminated the wearer's peripheral vision, so if approached by a hoodie-wearer on the street in a threatening fashion, it would be child's play to side-step the potential frontal assault by veering to the side, thus allowing one to achieve the advantageous posture to reign blows upon the side of the attacker's head and neck. Many a nefarious scheme to either mug us or interest us in a magazine subscription or car warranty extension would have been avoided with this approach. With crime-stopping policies such as stop-and-frisk, the hoodie's reputation changed somewhat during the 90s, becoming as vanilla and harmless as the once-gritty streets of Times Square in New York City.

But then 2012 happened, and an unarmed, Skittles-and-iced-tea bearing Trayvon Martin was shot to death while wearing a hoodie.

After that, the hoodie's association became a duality. On the one hand, the garment was improperly tinged as the outerwear of choice for Black hoodlums. But it also became emblematic of the Black Lives Matters movement. George Zimmerman's defense presented the hoodie argument, claiming that their defendant was correct in assuming a threat from the hoodie-wearing 17-year-old just heading home. Fox News mouthpiece, Geraldo Rivera, pleaded with young Black people to stop wearing hoodies, although he eventually apologized for the comment. *Dress Codes* author and law professor Richard Thompson Ford said, "As the hoodie became associated with 'Black hoodlums' in the media, some Black people avoided them and others embraced them: the public image of the hoodie made it into a statement of racial pride and defiance, solidarity with a community, an emblem of belonging, and all of that reinforced the negative associations for those who were inclined to be afraid of assertive Black people." That same year of 2012, Facebook Founder and CEO Mark Zuckerberg wore a hoodie for his company's initial public offering. In 2015, Oklahoma state representative Don Barrington proposed a bill criminalizing garments that he claimed attempted to conceal the wearer's identity, a thinly veiled accusation toward the hoodie and the minorities he felt wore them. Many were quick to accuse Barrington's comments as inherently racist. Because they were.

High schools began banning the hoodie, as its "gangsta" implications were very real to parents and authority figures. New England Patriots head coach Bill Belichick became associated with the hoodie when he first wore one on January 18, 2004, at the AFC championship game against the Indianapolis Colts, in a snow game won by the Patriots 24–14. Perhaps not as negative an association as gangsta rap, Belichick was also known as "Beli-cheat" for the many cheating scandals that he has been connected to during his tenure at New England. But there was no denying the impact of having Belichick—and even Tom Brady—wearing it. Millions of football fans adopted the gear to signify their support for laundry worn by members of their favorite sports team.

The hoodie has had a long and tortured history predating modern football gladiators and street urchins. Often associated with Medieval monks, they have become both fashion statements and protest garments. Worn by the likes of Justin Bieber, Little Red Riding Hood, Bill Belichick, The Grim Reaper, and Avril Lavigne, it has also graced the cover of Margaret Atwood's 1985 novel, *The Handmaid's Tale*, representing the oppression of women. But as is the case with our sartorial choices, what defines them is who wears them and under what circumstances. And that is what blew it for everybody. Had Ted Kaczynsky or Trayvon Martin worn a kimono, would that have turned it into a negative association, causing Pavlovian triggers of fear? If the media covered it that way, possibly. Maybe it's more about the head. Baseball caps worn backward caused a similar reaction in white people as did males wearing their pants hanging down below their butts. If somebody, *anybody,* approached you in a dark alley wearing their Yankee hat backwards and sagging pants, that should have elicited derision, and not knee-knocking fear. It's just clothes, or fashion, or whatever word helps you get through your day without needing to gobble down Xanax. Mafia members are known for wearing dark suits and ties, but that doesn't mean we should start plotzing when we attend funerals, formal weddings, or proms with satanic themes. Maybe some gangsta rapper or mugger out there can start a fad by wearing a Hello Kitty T-shirt while on stage or on the job in the streets of your neighborhood. Having the fight-or-flight instinct triggered by that emblem could actually have a positive result on society.

SAMBO'S

In 1957, a restaurant that was basically a knockoff of Denny's, opened with the name of Sambo's. The name came from the two owners, Sam Battistone and Newell Bohnett, but people naturally thought it was derived from the book *The Story of Little Black Sambo*. The founders decided to ride that wave into infamy and so decorated the walls with scenes from the book.

Not cool, dudes.

The latter half of the 70s saw the chain being pressured to change its name, even though the book, first published in 1899, was one of the first tomes to depict Black heroes in children's literature, which was sooo accepted by white America in the 70s. But in the 20th century, the character names were used as racial slurs, and the illustrations were drawn in pickaninny style, so yet another thing that started out actually representing progress was out the window. Even Saturday Night Live,

in their early years, poked fun at the chain by reporting, during their news segment, that they were going to change their name to Bob's Jew Boy to diffuse the furor, causing the Jewish Defense League (JDL) to put a horse's head in Dan Ackroyd's bed—but one that was blessed by a rabbi first, ensuring that it was Kosher. Protests against the restaurant popped up in Virginia, Connecticut, Rhode Island, Ohio, and Michigan. The owners held fast, insisting they had operated the 850 restaurants under the name for 20 years. It was a family restaurant, they said, and they weren't about to fiddle with success, and they gave them the finger (not really, but damn, they should have). The controversy grew, and it coincided with the chain's financial struggles in 1978–1979— which was due more to managerial and structural problems than its racist overtones, because why blame racists when you can point the finger at middle management? But the protests grew and the NAACP mounted challenges in multiple states, ignoring the fact that Sambo's actually employed more Black people than most other companies and restaurants at the time—but once you get your marching shoes on, it's hard to abandon the protest. The chain was still thought to be guilty of discrimination in the minds of many during that era. Many judges actually sided with the chain, citing first amendment rights, and they offered that protestors could carry signs and publish ads against them as part of *their* first amendment rights, but at least the second amendment was never invoked, as that amendment is prickly. Sambo's did alter the name in some midwestern cities to No Place Like Sam's and Jolly Tiger, although We Are No Longer Sambos just never took off. But the damage was baked in their proverbial pancakes and nothing seemed to stop their image from taking a hit. The financial problems stemmed more from their "fraction of the action" scheme, where managers were entitled to 20% of the stores' profits while employees were allowed to bid for a percentage of the remaining gains—a Ponzi scheme if ever there was one. Sambo's filed for Chapter 11 in 1981, and by 1984, all remaining locations had either been sold or shuttered—or converted to a bunch of pizza parlors named Luigi's with that typical, mustachioed Italian on their delivery box. But most people remember the implied racism of the chain's name, not the financial collapse due to a harebrained financial idea. The last remaining Sambo's kept the name until 2020, when the George Floyd murder apparently enlightened the store's owner, Chad Stevens—the grandson of one of the original founders—to finally change the restaurant's name to Chad's. For some reason, only preppies frequented that location.

The May 2020 murder of George Floyd set the dominos falling for corporate name changes. Eskimo Pie became Edy's Pie because of the racist stereotyping of the word "Eskimo." "Eskimo" came to be considered racist due to it being used by non-native colonizers as a term thought to indicate "eater of raw meat," meaning "barbaric and violent," and who wants to think of raw meat when eating ice cream covered in chocolate? The etymology of the word is actually unclear. One school of thought has it coming from the Latin word *excommunicati*, meaning the excommunicated ones, as the natives of the Canadian Arctic weren't Christians or even Jehovah's Witnesses. Other linguists' theories have the word derived from the French word *esquimaux*, meaning "one who nets snowshoes," which was actually a very accurate description of how Arctic natives built snowshoes. They did this by tightly weaving or netting sinew from caribou or other animals across a wooden frame, hopefully after the animals had shuffled off this mortal coil, because to think of the alternative is, well, unthinkable.

PepsiCo changed their long-standing name and figure of Aunt Jemima breakfast brands due to her origins as the Black mammy from 19th- and early 20th-century minstrel shows. The logo was created in 1890 after Nancy Green, a former slave and storyteller, cook, and missionary worker, who actually hated pancakes and preferred blintzes from the local Jewish deli. Green became the company spokeswoman until her death in 1923. The new name is Pearl Milling Company. Yummy.

So what does one do with Hattie McDaniel, the actress who was the first Black person to be nominated and win an Oscar? She won for her portrayal of Mammy in 1939's *Gone with the Wind*. Mammy was the maid for the southern plantation, Tara. Hattie had to actually work as a maid, as her pay as a singer, comedian, and actor was never enough to support her. For her audition, she showed up in her actual maid's outfit. There was much handwringing in bringing the book to the big screen because of certain chapters. One passage had the Ku Klux Klan portrayed as saviors for Scarlett O'Hara after she was attacked by Black men. The scene was deleted, as were uses of the N-word, but they did keep in the word "Darkie." But they also kept in the description "white trash," so the book was an equal-opportunity racist tome.

McDaniel was asked not to appear at the Atlanta opening due to their segregation laws. Clark Gable threatened to boycott unless she was able to attend. She convinced him to not blow it off, and she attended the Hollywood opening with her picture featured prominently in the program.

McDaniel's Oscar win demonstrated both a victory and defeat regarding race relations. It would be fifty years before another Black actor would win an Oscar, when Whoopi Goldberg won for *Ghost*. Should *Gone With the Wind* be celebrated for some of its progress, or condemned for maintaining the status quo in its depiction of race and slavery? The same can be said of replacing the name and logo of Aunt Jemima with Pearl Milling. Was it a win, or another case of blowing it—as in out of proportion? And our lonely eyes turn to Mrs. Butterworth whose visage, at this moment, is unchanged—although the parent company, Conagra, has promised to do so. B&G Foods released a similar announcement for Cream of Wheat.

Mars, Incorporated also reacted to the George Floyd killing by changing Uncle Ben's to Ben's Original. Gone is the elderly Black man in a bow tie. Uncle Ben's dates back to the 1940s. It came from an eponymous rice farmer from Texas, while the logo was based on Frank Brown, the head waiter at an exclusive Chicago eatery. While the imagery wasn't taken from slavery, it was still thought to be a tokenized version of Black life, and thus a racial stereotype. Somehow, the word "snowflake" seems to be appropriate right about now.

Native Americans have also been used for a variety of product marketing—and, of course, sports teams' names and logos. Land O'Lakes removed their Native American woman from their butter packages, and football's Washington Redskins ditched their truly offensive name and logo—as did baseball's Cleveland Indians, who will be known as the Cleveland Guardians and will do so without the horrific character of Wahoo adorning their uniforms.

Some names and images are so obviously racist and offensive, they had to go. Others, not so much. The difference between Aunt Jemima, Uncle Ben, and Cream of Wheat was, while they absolutely harken back to times of slavery, they didn't actually endorse it, and they certainly didn't fight for its existence. And that's the difference between them and the Confederate flag and Confederate statues that stand in the public square. Those iconic symbols actually fought *for* slavery. They stood not only for its existence, but for its maintenance. Many of the other symbols, such as Sambo's, Mammy, Aunt Jemima, and Uncle Ben, in some ways, represented a form of progress, although it certainly shouldn't be considered a total mystery why many within the Black community vehemently disagree. When it comes to change and social progress, many rightfully point to Martin Luther King's urgency of change back in 1963, when he wrote in his "Letter from Birmingham Jail" that the oppressor always says "Wait" and that "Wait" really meant "Never." There really was a lot of waiting before many offensive (to some) images were eradicated, but there is also an argument for, "when does it stop?" People's names can be considered offensive, so let's never name a boy Richard or William, as their nicknames are penis euphemisms. Girls' names such as April, May, and June should cease, as they are prejudicial towards colder months of the year. Amanda, Anita, and Ophelia should be outlawed, as they are often used to make ridiculous mocking phrases that beg name-owners to be bullied. Some names are offensive because they don't fit who or what they represent, such as the Utah Jazz. When they were located in New Orleans, "Jazz" was the perfect moniker, but in Utah, it defied logic. The Utah Salties might make more sense, but Salties, from the Great Salt Lake, could be construed as a part of the description of crackers, and there once was a baseball team called the Atlanta Crackers who became the minor league affiliate of the Atlanta Braves, when they were all part of the Irony League. The Utah "Mormons are Polygamists" makes more sense, but would certainly not be received warmly by the Church of LDS. The graphic designer or ad agency that could render exciting and easy-to-read logos of Mormons or Polygamists would earn their fees in gold. But the Polygamists would eventually be shortened to The Pollies or Polys, and then we're right back where we started with a name that invokes the word Cracker.

Native Americans have been so poorly represented that they should be given exceptions when naming some of their businesses. Perhaps a casino could be named The White Devil Casino or Peckerwood Casino or maybe even Casino Hillbilly. When it comes to dropping your kids' college funds, most wouldn't care what the place was called, but at least the tribal owners could get a chuckle out of watching all of the white traffic lining up at the slots under signage indicating the idiots' true heritage.

So we blew it, by either being too easily offended or not offended enough. At any rate, we are in the times of name-change rage, because we obviously needed the distraction from the cornucopia of real problems that rightly piss us off. With apologies to Spock: fascinating.

LEAF BLOWERS

Technically, the leaf blower was invented in 1947 when the Japanese company Kyoritsu Noki Company initiated it as a backpacker, fogger apparatus, because who hasn't felt the need to have a fogger that fits conveniently on your back?. The company changed their name to Echo in 1978 and finally to Duster-Mister, which is the name in use today, even though it sounds like a bad rap act. And as that year fits the criteria of this treatise, that is the year we are marking. Fudging dates for self-interest is as American as blaming others for your mistakes. Besides, it was discovered in the 70s that the blower minus the chemical container would be perfect for the temporary movement of leaf placement, and it was actually not introduced into the United States until the 70s, so all is well with the fundamental theory being presented.

California droughts in the 70s brought the leaf blower to trend mightily, as the use of water for a variety of clean-up purposes was banned. And it wasn't too long after that where the leaf blower became the favorite tool of landscapers and suburban dads all over the country.

There is nothing more American than the leaf blower. It works on fossil fuel and creates more noise than a hole-punched muffler on a classic muscle car revving its engine. Nothing defines American masculinity than polluting the air with the sounds of a petroleum-sourced fart machine, idling at a traffic stop. But most important, leaf blowers don't eliminate the problem; they just give the problem to someone who is not you by aerosolizing a fine patina of dust to land ever so gracefully on your freshly washed automobile, or to settle into the lungs of an asthmatic passerby, triggering a massive attack to add even more decibels into the formerly quiet, suburban air. By 1990, annual sales reached in excess of 800,000 units of the abominations. Yes, thanks to some rat bastard who so cleverly figured out how to reverse the airflow on a gas-powered vacuum cleaner, we all have to suffer the slings and arrows of increasing air and noise pollution.

Just how bad is it? The pollutants expelled by the gizmo have been linked to cancer, heart disease, and asthma. A 2011 study showed that the Non-Methane Volatile Organic Compounds (NMVOCs) emitted by a leaf blower operated for 30 minutes is equivalent to the amount produced by a Ford F-150 pickup truck that has driven from Texas to Alaska, or at least the noise emitted by the caterwauling of

the rednecks blasting and singing to their favorite country music tunes while making that drive. But as every infomercial states, "But wait, there's more!" It's not enough that the contraptions cause adverse health effects from the copious amounts of spewing carbon monoxide, nitrogen oxides, hydrocarbons. and particulates generated by the exhaust gas. Dust clouds raised by the airflow can contain such lovely entities for us to breathe in as mold, pesticides, and even animal fecal matter. And noise levels and sound pressure levels far exceed those by the National Institute for Occupational Safety and Health (NIOSH), which is why you have to yell instructions to your landscaper multiple times even when the device is off and there are no other sounds in the neighborhood.

Bans and stringent manufacturing codes were instituted and the nickel-cadmium, battery-powered leaf blowers now operate with zero emissions and a much lower volume. But the older, deafness- and coughing fits-inducing models still abound, much like the old, Swiss-cheese underwear that the majority of American men refuse to throw away.

Technological advances that reduced noise and lung pollution aside, the concept of the leaf blower hasn't changed: to take your shit and blow it onto someone else's property, thus making it their shit. The leaf blower wasn't even the first idea for passing the polluting buck. The smokestack and the dumping of industrial sewage into our waterways have been around for over a century. Take your problem and blow it or dump it elsewhere. Problem solved. While many laws have been enacted, repealed, and re-enacted, the problem remains. We blew it when we first accepted the idea of blowing something onto other people's property in the first place, be it smoke, industrial waste, or leaves.

SELF-SERVE

The latest trend is smart vending machines, which offer services such as cashless payments; face, eye, or fingerprint recognition; and social media connectivity. It is likely that vending machines of the future will recognize you and tailor their offerings to your interests and tastes. A beverage vending machine, for example, might recognize what you have purchased at other machines and ask you if you want your usual skim latte with a double shot of vanilla. And if you decide to be different that day, it will become your mother and serve you your perceived favorite, as it knows what its Bubbleah wants.

Market research shows 20 percent of all vending machines are smart machines, with at least 3.6 million units knowing who you are and what you like—which is much more than we can say for ourselves. Take me to a restaurant whose menu is more than a single page and I end up weeping in the corner, curled up in the fetal position, as too many choices puts me right back in the womb.

This sounds like a good thing, almost a utopia where the machines we build know us intimately and thus so many of our mundane business transactions can be done without the inconvenience of personal contact with human beings or even having to make up our minds. The customer will always be right, as the robot vending machine will have all our algorithms to choose our favorites. Our occasional brain farts or wishy-washy behavior won't cause the person behind us to throw a hissy fit. What could possibly go wrong?

Vending, or automatic retailing, has been around since the late 19th century, with stamps being the primary, original product. In 1897, vending machines featuring Tutti-Frutti Gum were installed on elevated subway platforms in New York—or you could just go to the underside of any fifth grade student's school desk and have your choice of any number of flavored gums. Gumballs followed in 1907, and we've been tripping on sidewalks ever since. Horn & Hardart had the first automat, which became very popular during The Depression as if you didn't have enough money to buy food—at least you could watch the poor saps get their food out of a giant storage bin. 1926 saw the first cigarette vending machines, and in the 1930s, bottled soda vending machines were introduced, causing an immediate rise in both cancer and gas. 1967 produced the first canned soda vending machine,

although the first actual soda vending machine appeared in the 1920s, which dispensed soda into a paper cup—or tried to. More often than not, it just served as a funnel to get the soda on the floor or your shoes.

So we can get soda, cigarettes, and gum—to help hide the bad breath caused from cigarettes—from vending machines in the 60s. What else could be made more convenient?

Gasoline.

"There is growing recognition in the petroleum industry that the auto has revolutionized all retailing—except the retailing of the gas station! It is even seeping into the awareness of this industry that car traffic is now shopping traffic, and that more cars, driven by men as well as women, stop at gas stations every day than drive up to any other outlet, including perhaps the food outlet! No other retailer so completely wastes such a remarkable traffic count as does the gas station!"

—Legendary advertising and marketing executive E.B. Weiss in the 1964 book, Management and the Marketing Revolution

So in 1964, John Roscoe, who owned a chain of convenience stores in Colorado, flipped the switch on his first row of self-serve pumps—and we're to assume that the switch actually worked, otherwise, it would be pointless to mention it. Soon, he became licensed to sell the box that Herbert Timms invented that allowed an attendant inside the convenience store to dispense the gas at the pumps. But other retailers were reluctant—because they were obviously vehemently against making money, a first for anyone in the oil and gas industry. First, there were fire codes that prevented self-service dispensers; those regulations allowing the remote dispensers gradually passed in 48 states. But the concept still didn't catch fire—pun intended—by the pre-1969, line-in-the-sand date.

But then, in 1973 and 1974, the gas shortage caused by OPEC nations to embargo countries that supported Israel in the 1973 Yom Kippur War caused prices to spike four-fold, and long lines at the pumps ensued (because the Jewish Space Lasers hadn't been deployed yet). You had no idea what the price per gallon was until you actually made it to the front of the line, causing the law stating that gas stations had to show their prices in easy-to-see signage, that rarely corresponded to the PR. And convenience stores that had no fealty to any one gasoline brand began installing pumps to sell unbranded gasoline, which was cheaper than name brands. But some convenience stores still resisted, fearing long lines at their registers would mean less store-only patrons would come in. That problem was alleviated in the 80s, when credit card readers were integrated into the pumps. In 1973, only 13 percent of convenience stores sold gasoline. Today, that number is 80 percent.

So what else was the result of the idea of self-service that took seed in the 19th century and exploded in the last 50 years? In the oil/gas industry, thousands of guys named Bob—who wore their name on their greasy overalls and happily asked you if they should "Fill 'er up" and "check under the hood" while squeegeeing your windows clean, checking your tire pressure, and removing the oil dipstick to wipe it down with a greasier rag to see just where you stood on how much oil your grocery-go-getter was burning—were out of work. In the spring of 2020, fuel demand cratered 40 percent due to Covid, and other industries that had been experimenting with self-serve started to accelerate it, as human interaction not only proved to be expensive, but deadly. Movie theaters, which have long desired to eliminate employees from their chain model, had gone to ticket kiosks and promoting online sales to avoid what used to be lines, but now that was just a way to avoid the virus from crossing from their teenaged fingers to your immune-compromised hands. They installed freestyle soda machines so you could get your own, damn, five-hundred-ounce drink, and other concessions were being sold at various vending machines. Airlines had also been using ticket kiosks rather than have you wait in the Disneyland-styled obstacle course lines to get your ticket. Self-serve at the grocery store checkout now had the lines, while the few employees standing at the end of the mini conveyor belts stood lonely and bored and in much fewer numbers. So you picked out, checked out, and bagged your own food, eliminating a single human response during your weekly sojourn to the Piggly Wiggly. The most coveted job these days is the delivery driver, be it pizza, groceries, or everything you bought online at Amazon. Self-serve morphed into just "self." All one needs is a phone app and a credit card, PayPal, or Venmo to get everything one needs. It's just too much bother and far too dangerous to venture out, even if it's just to go someplace with a vending machine to get our food, drinks, or cancer sticks. Why not have self-serve massage parlors? At least then you're guaranteed a happy ending.

Is this really better?

And most self-serve equipment, if they aren't already, will be built in automated factories, eliminating more people from actually being able to buy the things they no longer need to go outside for. As we already know about the future of vending machines being smart apps that know what we want, how long before everything that delivers our necessities will be built with that app, negating the need to even use our phones or laptops to put in an order? Everything we want and need will be automatically delivered, because it will know when we need it. The irony is that the formerly named "convenience store" won't resemble anything that we consider "convenient," and will disappear, as the shopping mall has. Self-driving cars will stop at self-service gas stations that won't need to be part of the ancient idea of a convenience store. All domiciles will have some form of off-loading transportation method to deliver our goods directly to whatever portal desired. And if evolution has taught us anything, we can imagine what parts of our bodies won't be needed anymore and should start disappearing soon, if they haven't already, beginning with the gray matter inside our skulls. How much more "blowing it" can you get?

SO IT'S REALLY BLOWN?

At the end of Martin Scorsese's *Goodfellas*, Ray Liotta's Henry Hill looks at the camera and says, "We ran everything. We paid off cops. We paid off lawyers. We paid off judges. Everybody had their hands out. Everything was for the taking. And now it's all over."

He could have been talking about American Exceptionalism, or The American Experiment, or whatever you want to call it. AE was a simple premise: a rejection of the European monarchies and their Great Regimes of Lords and Peons, with the Peons working the Lord's land to ensure that they stay rich and were able to "lord it" over the rest of them. It was supposed to create a constitutional Republic where everyone would be equal, with the exception of Blacks, women, and those pesky indigenous people. So right out of the gate, the Experiment was blown—or at least half-blown. Over the next several centuries, there were constant upheavals in the system with wars, internal struggles, assassinations, greed, and malfeasance, but also not without some good ideas being implemented. The past 50-plus years have been a microcosm of all that. We fought and struggled both outside and inside our borders, and while the country was our patient, and we worked diligently to keep it alive after massive coronaries, strokes, and cancers, post-operative infections snuck in through tiny paper cuts and left the patient on life support.

It's often said, "don't sweat the small stuff," and "everything is small stuff," which is exactly the point. Big stuff makes the headlines and takes up most of our head space, but the small stuff is everywhere, happening every day, and it becomes such a part of the fabric of our existence that we fail to connect the dots to see how it caused death by a thousand cuts.

The Founding Fathers worked to create a system based on the premise that if you want a strong system, divide everything. And it worked. We are as divided a system as you could have planned. We have been one, long Hatfield–McCoy feud. The names and arguments change over time, but the feud never stops. So maybe the Experiment is over, and everybody wants to shut the lab down—or at least discover where the leak is.

Some people look at The Experiment as if it were a computer that crashed and want to reboot it back to a time where they felt everything worked. They think the Status Quo was great when only a certain type of person actually had any status. It's that pervasive attitude that has made the AE susceptible to fraying at the edges rather than from a frontal assault.

So it's on life support. We're on life support. We've had the usual upheavals that we have endured in the prior centuries—war, disease, political malfeasance, environmental issues, social issues, immigration issues, even terrorism, but lately we've also been subjected to the form of water torture where a single, repeated drop of water splashes onto our foreheads, driving us totally and irreparably mad. Or we've been out stubbing our toe to forget how much our head hurts. History hasn't been kind to Democracies; their death rattles are slow, painful, and protracted. You rarely see it coming, as the bitterness between rival factions interferes with any thought about the collective good. Religion and spirituality clash until both are unrecognizable, and trying to trace down all the threads of how we got here was like Popeye Doyle chasing the drug dealer through the streets of New York. But our problems won't end with a shot in the back on an elevated train's stairwell. Popeye did become an addict in the sequel, so, perhaps the metaphor is perfect.

Yes, it all sounds hyperbolic. And a lot of it is, which is why many of these essays read more like satire, or at least the reminiscing of two life partners saying to each other, "Remember the time when we almost killed each other? That's so funny now." Maybe we can get to that point and avoid riding up to the decapitated head of the Statue of Liberty and then dropping to our knees and railing to the heavens. Yes, God damn us to Hell, every one.

So where do we stand? Having blown big stuff, small stuff, and everything in between, has the tipping point finally been reached where, similar to what scientists are predicting regarding climate change, all we can do is put on the brakes but it won't prevent us from eventually hurtling over the cliff? Is there no way where Billy can say, "We did it" and the rest of us respond, "That's Goddamn right!" Or are we all so lacking in inner warmth that it's shocking that we haven't collectively hugged a furnace to death?

The evolution of life comes as an inevitable consequence of a certain amount of time on a planet in a stable orbit which is not too hot or too cold. First comes chemical evolution—chance rearrangements of basic matter, then biological evolution.

Maybe we're just waiting for the monoliths to arrive and propel us to a new level of evolution—toward anywhere our neural pathways aren't hardwired to always blow it. We can speculate about the philosophical, physiological, neurological, or any other -ological regarding where we came from, where we are, and where we are heading, but what isn't known is if we will actually emerge. Will we be a Star Child that the Monolith will have brought us through to another side, another life, another...chance?

We've been blowing it for over 50 years, probably for over six million years, and we'll probably blow it for another six million more.

But whatever we do, we'll do it together, be that our continued proclivity to blow it or, maybe someday, to do something different.

We're all on this spinning orb together. Of course there's no accounting for taste, especially among tourists.

IMAGE CREDITS

Barbostick. "Ferris Bueller boat." Wikimedia Commons, 25 July 2009, https://commons.wikimedia.org/wiki/File:Ferris_Bueller_boat_(3756307743).jpg. Creative Commons Attribution-Share Alike 2.0 Generic License.

Bill Oakley. "Conan O'Brien 1992" Wikimedia Commons, 22 May 2008, https://commons.wikimedia.org/wiki/File:Conan_O%27Brien_1992.jpg. GNU Free Document License.

"Boblurts." Wikimedia Commons, 1 Oct. 1972, https://commons.wikimedia.org/wiki/File:Boblurts.jpg. Public Domain.

Capricorn Records. "The Allman Brothers Band (1972)." Wikimedia Commons, 1972, https://commons.wikimedia.org/wiki/File:The_Allman_Brothers_Band_(1972).JPG. Public Domain.

Cbaile19. "Leaf Blower, Homewood Cemetery." Wikimedia Commons, 3 Nov. 2014, https://commons.wikimedia.org/wiki/File:Leaf_blower,_Homewood_Cemetery.jpg. Creative Commons CC0 1.0 Universal Public Domain Dedication.

Christopher Ziemnowicz. "1971 AMC Gremlin AMO 2015 show - all original 1of6." Wikimedia Commons, 25 July 2015, https://commons.wikimedia.org/wiki/File:1971_AMC_Gremlin_AMO_2015_show_-_all_original_1of6.jpg. CC BY 4.0.

Doge24190. "Nike Dunk Low Retro "Varsity Green"." Wikimedia Commons, 15 June 2021, https://commons.wikimedia.org/wiki/File:Nike_Dunk_Low_Retro_%-22Varsity_Green%22.jpg. Creative Commons Attribution-Share Alike 4.0 International license.

Federal Bureau of Investigation agents. "Hooded jacket found among Ted Kaczynski's belongings." Wikimedia Commons, circa 1996, https://commons.wikimedia.org/wiki/File:Hooded_jacket_found_among_Ted_Kaczynski%27s_belongings.jpg. Public Domain.

Ian Muttoo. "Have It Your Way." Wikimedia Commons, 8 Jan. 2009, https://commons. wikimedia.org/wiki/File:Have_It_Your_Way_(3237101971).jpg. Creative Commons Attribution-Share Alike 2.0 Generic license.

Mike Morbeck. "Colin Kaepernick (cropped headshot)." Wikimedia Commons, 9 Sept. 2012, https://commons.wikimedia.org/wiki/File:Colin_Kaepernick_(cropped_headshot).jpg. Creative Commons Attribution-Share Alike 2.0 Generic license.

"MTV-black." Wikimedia Commons, https://commons.wikimedia.org/wiki/File:MTV-black.svg. Public Domain.

NASA. "SH Minimum Ozone." Wikimedia Commons, https://commons.wikimedia.org/wiki/File:SH_Minimum_Ozone.png. Public Domain.

National Enquirer. "National Enquirer logo 2014." Wikimedia Commons, 15 Nov. 2021, https://commons.wikimedia.org/wiki/File:National_Enquirer_logo_2014.svg. Public Domain.

NBC. "Saturday Night Live logo." Wikimedia Commons, est. 2005, https://commons.wikimedia.org/wiki/File:Saturday_Night_Live_logo.jpg. Public Domain.

RMY Auctions. "Arnold Schwarzenegger 1974." Wikimedia Commons, 1974, https://commons.wikimedia.org/wiki/File:Arnold_Schwarzenegger_1974.jpg. Public Domain.

Sambo's Restaurants, Inc. "Sambo's" Wikimedia Commons, 1 Sept. 1981, https://commons.wikimedia.org/wiki/File:Sambo%27s.png. CC-Zero Public Domain.

Sony Pictures. "The Social Network." Wikimedia Commons, 2010, https://commons.wikimedia.org/wiki/File:The_Social_Network.jpg. CC-Zero Public Domain.

United States Marshals Service. "Eddie Antar mugshot.png." Wikimedia Commons, 27 Feb. 1990, https://commons.wikimedia.org/wiki/File:Eddie_Antar_mugshot.png. Public Domain.

ABOUT THE AUTHOR

Barry R. Norman has been a media junkie, having worked for magazines, newspapers, television (with stints at CNN, Professional Wrestling, Cartoon Network and six Olympic Games), radio as the co-creator of a nationally, syndicated, alternative show and film. He is an award-winning filmmaker, film festival founder/executive director, and owned and operated a movie theater in Brunswick, Maine. Barry is currently working as a full-time substitute teacher in the Everett, MA school system. *We Blew It* is his 6th book. Coming up soon - his 7th book, *Counting Kitties: A Guide for the Modern Insomniac.*